FACES

OF A

NEIGHBORHOOD

FACES
OF A
NEIGHBORHOOD

Boston's South End in the
Early Twenty-first Century

—

LYNNE POTTS

ISBN-13: 978-1537705569
ISBN-10: 1537705563

Contact: lynnepotts@lynnepotts.com
DESIGNED BY SAM POTTS

lh LOCAL HISTORY PUBLISHERS

PRINTED IN THE UNITED STATES.

CONTENTS

FACES

OF A

NEIGHBORHOOD

INTRODUCTION

IN WINTER, when evening is falling over the city, I like to
walk the streets of Boston's South End, looking in windows
where shades or drapes have not yet been drawn against the
night. In this neighborhood of brick row houses, you can see
into dining rooms and kitchens on the street floors and into
living rooms on the parlor-level at the top of front stoop. If it's
almost dinner hour, someone may be cooking or setting the
table, sometimes children are playing on the floor, occasionally a teen is slouched on a couch with an iPhone. Because I
can see some houses in their early twentieth-century condition, some reconfigured into apartments, and some restored to
single-family homes with all the latest features and furnish-
ings, I'm able to observe various living styles. For example,
in some houses the old fluourescent lighting still exists; in
others, track lighting has been installed; in still others crystal
chandeliers hang from eleven-foot ceilings that cast light over
lush couches and Oriental rugs.

Whichever interior I happen to see, I am invariably curious about the people who live there. If I could actually see their faces I would surely recognize some, having passed them in Titus Sparrow Park or in the aisles of Shaw's Market. Even so, I would wonder how they spend their days, what has been important to them, what has made them proud or sad—and what the neighborhood means to them.

When I asked myself what prompted this curiosity, I realized it came from my past—a long-standing feeling I had of wanting to *belong* in the place where I lived. I grew up in a Detroit suburb and, like many Midwesterners who rebelled against its cheerful provincialism, I was eager to get out. Detroit had a flourishing pop and jazz scene, major league sports teams, and an established museum, but I lived on the sterile fringes. My mother spent her days shopping for groceries, picking up laundry at the cleaners, and taking us to church and school activities. My father had a business downtown, but that didn't mean I had access to the city. By my early teens, I was dying to leave.

The summer after college graduation, I packed up my Ford Falcon (a Detroit girl after all) and moved to New York for more schooling and the adventure of living in a great metropolitan city. After a couple of years, however, I thought I'd try Boston—maybe settle where I had college friends and where the scale wasn't so grand. It didn't work out that way. I met a man who was volunteering at a Beacon Hill school where I taught third grade, married him the next year, and the two of us moved to Berkeley, California, where he began a Ph.D. program and I began teaching in a high school.

Those were heady days in the United States, but Berkeley seemed particularly stirred up with social and political change: the Free Speech movement on the University of California campus, Black Panthers in Oakland, anti-Vietnam protests in the streets, and psychedelic drugs in Haight-Ashbury. We were swept up in the whirlwind of it all—but when Sam was born and I was pregnant again, my husband and I decided to leave. A graduate degree in English seemed less relevant all the time, and we wanted to escape the evils of the *military-industrial complex* to live in the country as many of our peers were doing. When friends in New York asked us to join them on a Vermont dairy farm they had just purchased with money from their townhouse wedding present, we thought it was a perfect plan.

The hills on the western slope of the Green Mountains were full of young people like us in the 1970s—dreamy-eyed couples who planned to "live off the land," read books in the evening, and work on their respective arts in their spare hours. We lasted ten months on the dairy farm and barely made it through another two and a half years on our own desolate farm near Lake Champlain before it all collapsed. The second winter everyone, except baby Emmy, got pneumonia, the Ford pickup broke down, and the spring garden was ravaged by a plague of woodchucks. A few hippie friends joined us in various living rooms to bulk-order food from the regional co-op, but we could hardly say we had a neighborhood. When my husband and I moved to Boston separately, I desperately wanted to settle somewhere I could call home.

I knew about the South End from days attending St. Stephen's Church on Shawmut Avenue when I was teaching those earlier years on Beacon Hill. Familiar with the neighborhood, I started looking for an apartment, finally finding one I could afford on West Rutland Square. The walls of the building had separated from the living room floor so snow blew in through the bricks during winter storms and I had to keep moving the Volkswagen because its wooden bumpers were illegal, but I was grateful to be in a place where I could imagine fitting in at some point. The children and I lived in that apartment for a year and a half until I found an aging Holyoke Street rooming house for sale, took a loan out on the Vermont barn roof, and bought the house in 1978.

The next ten to fifteen years I worked as a freelance writer during the day, was mother and cook in the afternoon and evenings, and was a house-wrecker at night. I tore down false walls, stripped mustard-yellow paint off woodwork and stairs, and tore up linoleum by the fistfuls to be carted away in discarded liquor store boxes by city trash trucks. Gradually I identified the best supermarket for us, registered the children at the South End Community Health Clinic, learned the various school options, and started to frequent the South End branch of the Boston Public Library. Soon the children were involved with school activities and I was busy with work. The years slipped by without any major disasters but I still didn't feel at home.

Then, in the mid-1990s, when the children were off to

college, I began reading any history of the South End I could find—the people who had first settled the area in the 1860s and those who came in the following decades. After reading, I began researching threads of the story in city archives and historical societies, finally writing a local history called *A Block in Time: History of Boston's South End Through a Window on Holyoke Street.*

Knowing more, however, did not make me feel any more at home. Fortunately, I was rescued one spring morning when Al Destra from the Food Emporium on Columbus Avenue stopped me to ask if I was going to do another book about the South End. His question, along with starting to meet neighbors in my community garden, at South End library events, and in weekly meetings of the South End Seniors, made me think another writing project might be a good idea. Reflecting on those winter-evening walks when I wondered about the people on the other side of lighted windows, I settled on a plan to interview several current South Enders and ask them to talk about their lives and how they felt about the neighborhood.

It was tricky. I didn't know if I could find people willing to speak with me, and I wasn't sure their stories would come together in any way that would interest readers. Still, having spent so much time on its history, I thought it would be interesting to explore the neighborhood at this moment in time.

Eventually, I found twenty-four people willing to meet. Curiously, most were not only willing to talk candidly about their lives, but also about how they felt about living where they did. Most shared my desire to belong, or at least to make sense of why they had chosen it for their home, but some were dissatisfied and critical. It would all be part of the story.

— • —

I begin with Elna Rapp who moved to the South End in the 1980s when many of the neighborhood's old rooming houses were being converted into apartments and condominiums. Elna had been renting on Beacon Hill when a mutual friend suggested she contact me to learn what her options might be in the South End. Once she had purchased and moved to Holyoke Street, Elna and I developed a casual friendship, the kind that comes with commiserating over pesky problems on the block: non-functioning street lights, broken tree limbs after a storm, vacant garden plots, the lowered water table, stray cats, etc. She stored her bicycle in my downstairs foyer for a while, and I was her guest for tea a couple of times, but I had never had a chance to put the pieces of her life together until we met for the purposes of this book.

Elna Rapp

Elna Rapp wears her hair pulled back in a bun revealing sculpted features, hazel eyes, and a shy, coquettish smile. Her apartment is modestly furnished with Shaker-style tables and sparsely arranged rugs, and if you were to have tea with her some late afternoon, she would serve it from a silver teapot in Limoge China cups accompanied by cucumber sandwiches (crusts removed), deviled eggs, and slices of fresh tomato. The sweet at the end would be from L.A. Burdick Handmade Chocolates in Harvard Square, to which Elna would have pedaled on her bike to buy.

But don't be fooled. Under the exterior of refinement and good taste, there's a strong, independent spirit. I didn't say *fierce*, but definitely a person with a mind of her own. The bicycle is a case in point. While many South Enders maneuver their way to the market or hardware store in sedans or SUVs on a winter day, Elna is bundled up, riding in the fresh air with the front basket full. It is not just to be economical, which she religiously is, but because it is more efficient and environmentally correct. Bicycles make sense, Elna says. Why care if some people consider them impractical, even dangerous? They are the best transportation for city living—easy, fast, and fuel free. Her bicycle, by the way, is a hand-built Pashley, shipped by special order from Stratford-on-Avon, England. It's a world-recognized classic; you could say it's the Bentley of the bicycle world.

Elna moved to the South End in 1986 when her Beacon Hill landlord was going to sell her apartment in his building. Since all kinds and sizes of condos were being developed in the South End at the time, she said it was easy to find one she liked. The choice was important because she wanted her new home to be a *permanent* home.

Elna was born near Richmond, Virginia, where her father had been sent to a Quaker alternative service camp as a conscientious objector during World War II. After the war, the family moved to New Haven, Connecticut, where her father studied for a graduate degree in forestry. Finished with that, he moved the family to Costa Rica, where he worked as manager of a balsa mill. Five years later, the family moved to a farmhouse in Rockland County, New York, where her father worked for a lumber supplier until the mid-1950s, when he decided they should move to Mexico.

"I was in middle school when we went to Mexico but the British school I attended stopped in tenth grade so my parents sent me to Switzerland for my junior year and then to a Quaker school in Pennsylvania for my senior year. By that time, I was pretty much on my own and I guess all the moving explains, to some extent, my wanting to make the South End permanent. I think it's good to have roots in a place. My parents moved so often they really never got to know anyone well. I wanted to live a different way," Elna said.

Despite all the changes, Elna developed a steadfast passion for dance. While the family was living in New York, she fell in love with ballet, eventually taking classes at the Juilliard School and at the Martha Graham School on 63rd Street. She auditioned for New York's High School of Performing Arts and was accepted, but the move to Mexico preempted that. Still determined, however, she returned to New York for another session at the Martha Graham School and later arranged to study with a prima ballerina in Mexico. Unfortunately, schooling in Switzerland brought that to an end, and after graduation from high school, she applied to Pratt Institute in New York to study graphic design. The chance to be a dancer had passed.

The year she completed Pratt, she took a design job for Hallmark Cards in Kansas City, Missouri, for a year, but she returned to New York where she could continue her career in design and pursue her interests in art, early music, and English country dancing. In 1968, ready to leave New York and thinking she might like Boston, Elna took a train there, booked a room at the Y, and started looking for work, eventually settling on a graphic design job at Little, Brown Publishing Company.

Though Elna settled in Boston, she did not stay in graphic

design. After a few years she decided to go into nursing, apply-ing to the program at Massachusetts General Hospital for her training, graduating first in her class, and happy to start a new career in "almost mid-life," she said. "Nursing school was hard, then. We were some of the last to be educated the old-fashioned way—wearing black shoes, black stockings, and white uniforms that had to be taken apart piece by piece so they could be starched stiff and run through a mangle iron." Her first job was with a large ophthalmology practice, special-izing in treatment for the retina. She stayed at that job for fifteen years.

A story I knew about Elna revealed a great deal about her character and personality, so I asked her to repeat it for me. In the early 2000s, she was among a group of South Enders who learned that a lowered water table threatened to dry the pil-ings supporting their treasured Victorian bowfronts. Elna told me she knew of three Holyoke buildings where contractors had to remove rotted pilings before they could begin renova-tions. As the owner of a unit next to one of these houses, she decided to find out if her building was at risk. "I had to per-suade the other co-op members, but I was hell-bent on find-ing out, even though I knew we would have to get it fixed if the report was positive. And it would be very expensive!" Nev-ertheless, with her singular tenacity and persuasive powers, Elna convinced fellow owners they needed the study, which, indeed, showed rotted pilings. "We were unusual because we were living in the building while the excavating was going on, but we got through it."

The task was particularly complicated because the owner of the basement floor apartment was a compulsive collector of alley debris: newspapers, books, discarded garden pots, knickknacks, file cabinets, broken chairs, telephones, mirrors, an occasional computer—an endless list. The owner had to move out for the work to be done. It was Elna who cajoled and finally physically moved the basement owner, in taxis and borrowed cars, to the local YWCA. "I had to do all the packing to put her things in storage. It wasn't easy."

Now retired, Elna stays busy volunteering at the Athenæum and at the Animal Rescue League in the South End. She loves animals, especially cats. "I was besotted with cats from when I was very young," she said, smiling at her use of the archaism. "All my life I've loved them, but I didn't really get into working with them until I retired. Now I go to the Animal Shelter on Chandler Street two or three days a week for about two hours, often filling in for regular staff on holidays as well."

She has a second volunteer engagement that taps into the old passion she never lost. Three times a week during performance seasons, Elna works in a backstage studio at the Boston Ballet Company. Her task is to help sew and individually fit garments to the dancers. "Some outfits are rented, others are brought from storage, and some are new, but they always have to be fitted so the dancers have perfect freedom to move," she explained. When I asked if she had worked on the *Nutcracker* costumes this year, she said, "Oh yes, there's a dance with Chinese dancers dressed in beautiful Chinese fabrics. I've been picking up scraps of satin, taffeta, tulle, and lace from the floor to bring home for use." Then she told me she made cards that were sold in the Ballet gift shop. Did I want one?

Later that day, Elna arrived at my office with a #7 envelope containing a blank vellum greeting card. On the front of the card was the cut-out of a ballerina over a piece of fabric—a dark green and gold appliqué piece of Chinese silk. I couldn't help but note how design and dance came together in this artful creation.

— • —

I knew Victor Howes in much the same way I knew Elna. We met in the 1980s and our paths crossed occasionally after that. Victor and I had both been members of a writing group that met in a space that the Community Church rented on Boylston Street, but I had never had a chance to speak with him at length. I saw him from time to time walking on Tremont Street, but I didn't know why he had settled in the South End or anything about his life. This is what I discovered.

Victor Howes

Victor Howes doesn't tell you where he went to college or where he got his Ph.D. You have to ask him directly to learn about his career as an English professor and as a poet. In short, he is a gentleman—accomplished, distinguished, but totally uninterested in impressing others.

Even back in the days of the Boylston group, Victor's poems had a whimsicality that drew me to them. While not always humorous, they revealed a sharp wit, usually masterfully honed in the last line. Here's one of my favorites, a cleverly executed Shakespearean sonnet:

Porcupine

Prickly, standoffish, lumbering, he comes
To lick the salt I set out for the cattle.
He comes when no one's looking; he assumes
His paw-prints tell no tales, and cows don't tattle.

Not that I need to know. He's not the kind
For sociability. A feudal fort
Minus the moat is what he brings to mind,
Bristling with spears, a pike at every port.
He won't allow us to be better friends.
I call him Mr. Spiny, but it's hard
To get to first names. Conversation ends
Before it starts. I greet him. He's on guard.
Well, porcupine, O.K. At your insistence,
You keep the salt, I'll keep the friendly distance.

When we met, Victor told me that many of the people we used to meet with are now members of the New England Poetry Club that meets in the Harvard-Yenching Library on Divinity Avenue in Cambridge. He is retired, he said, and is a regular member of the Club.

Victor grew up and went to schools from first grade through twelfth in Malden, Massachusetts. It was a time, he said, when children ran free in their neighborhood. He felt like he grew up mostly outdoors—riding bikes, playing games, meeting with friends. Besides the freedom of living in a small town, he spent summers in the outdoors of Cape Cod.

After graduating high school in 1940, Victor went to college for two years before he interrupted his schooling to join the Navy. Feeling the urgency of World War II already underway, he enlisted and was told, after taking special tests, he qualified for a special V-12 Program training young men to be ensigns and officers. The enrollees eventually took special

Columbia University courses to prepare them for their new commanding positions. They became, in fact, known as the "Ninety Day Wonders" for the speed with which they acquired the requisite knowledge and skills to become leaders.

Although he never saw direct combat, Victor was sent to the South Pacific on a Landing Craft Tank (LCT), a ship used to carry supplies from the big ships to the shore—everything from food and drinks to bombs. Memories from those years were random and often amusing, he said, but one he often recalled was his company having tamed a goat and a monkey to live on the ship. The monkey eventually turned difficult and mean, Victor said, "but the goat, of course, just stayed a goat."

After the war ended in 1945, the Army retained Victor for a while, first in San Francisco and then in Washington, D.C. The Great Depression was not far in the past, he explained, and the government wanted to be sure these young men could get jobs when they got out. He liked Washington, D.C., and thought about staying but met a girl there and when the two married, they decided to come back to New England. Living in a large house on Beacon Hill where they rented out rooms, Victor was able to finish his undergraduate degree at Harvard College.

He taught for a while at Norwich University in Vermont— "a kind of military academy in those days"—but, on the advice of a colleague, applied and was accepted into Yale University's doctoral program in English. In his last year there he consulted a posted list of colleges and universities with openings for an English professor. "Northeastern was just starting to be well known, and I liked Boston, so when I applied and got the position, I was pleased," he said.

That was in 1959. Victor taught at Northeastern until retiring in 1991. More than equipped to take on a range of subjects, he eventually taught Shakespeare, American literature, history of English literature, Greek tragedies, modern poetry, and more. It was a full and rewarding career, but when he had the opportunity to retire, he took it. "I was ready to have some leisure time and enjoy life." Poetry was on his mind.

When I asked Victor why he had chosen literature and poetry as his life's work, he said both his parents had always loved to read. His mother read to him from an early age, adding without irony that his favorite book was *Little Women*. He had ideas for poems when he was very little, he said, and wrote his first one about a cat. His first published poem appeared in the Beebe Junior High School Bulletin when he was in the eighth grade. By the time he was a high school senior, the yearbook editors gave him the moniker, "Class Poet."

Victor didn't write much poetry in college, but he did at Yale. His dissertation on imitations of Horace by the eighteenth century English satirist Alexander Pope prompted him to write again and send out his work. Then, when some faculty members and graduate English students formed a group to share poems, he joined them. Thoroughly enjoying the exchange, he kept writing, with several hundred poems appearing in publications that included *The New York Times*, *The Christian Science Monitor*, *Classical Outlook*, and *Light*

Magazine. His chapbook *The Lobsterman's Daughter* was published by Northeastern University Press in 1969.

I asked Victor how he happened to buy a South End house in 1969 when the neighborhood was still run-down and dangerous. He told me he had lived in rented apartments in the Fenway and Watertown, but one day a secretary in the English department at Northeastern told him about a house in the South End that the Boston Redevelopment Authority (BRA) owned on Cazenove Street. A group of students had bought it for $6,000 and sold it for the same price after they graduated, essentially living free. When Victor heard the story, he began checking BRA records to see the agency's plans for similar properties. He learned about a brick bowfront on West Newton Street that he could get for $17,500 and promptly bought it.

Like many others who lived in the South End in the 1960s, Victor had stories of neighborhood life. Even I, coming to the South End in the 1970s, remember the legendary Mrs. Sheets and her many children—several of her own and others she fostered. Mr. Sheets had a disposal business, cleaning out abandoned or renovated houses, selling much of what he collected in a store he owned on Massachusetts Avenue. "Everyone knew the parents and most of the children. We used to call them Sheets and all the little ones pillowcases," Victor said. "They were very visible."

Victor still lives in the house he bought in the 1960s, but he has made many improvements—patching and painting, replacing old cupboards and doors, upgrading appliances, and endlessly mending broken fixtures. It wasn't his cup of tea, he said, but he did it. This poem describes his sentiments.

Handyman

Under my thumb all thumbtacks bend,
Brads buckle, penny-nails collapse.
A hinge I take an hour to mend
Stays mended half an hour, perhaps.
My tables rock, my faucets leak,
My doorknobs spin in empty space,
I plane, I plumb, I twist, I tweak,
I glue together, bolster, brace.
But what I plane is planed too short,
Or what I plumb is plumbed too loose.
I tweak a thing; it's tweaked too tight.
I glue with stick-proof, gum-less glues.
Which leads me to conclude that I
Was made for leisure and repose.
Things in their nature break, I sigh,
And contemplate that fact, and doze.

— • —

Elna and Victor both made deliberate decisions to move to the South End for practical reasons: Elna finally to settle in a Boston neighborhood; Victor to take advantage of a real estate bargain when he was teaching at Northeastern. Both had made new homes in the neighborhood when they were adults. Winnie Lowery's story was the opposite, that of a native South Ender who has lived her whole life in the neighborhood. In this way, she was almost unique among those I interviewed.

Winifred Lowery

Winifred "Winnie" Lowery was living in the Methunion Manor buildings on Columbus Avenue when I contacted her by phone. She suggested we meet at the Harriet Tubman House at 566 Columbus Avenue as she often had lunch there, though she had a second reason she would reveal when we met. It turns out that, for the first eleven years of her life, Winnie lived in the building that used to be where the Harriet Tubman House is now. In those days, she said, the house was right next door was the Hi Hat, one of the South End's most popular jazz clubs in the 1940s and 1950s. She had strong ties to the location!

Winnie's parents, herself and a brother, lived on the fourth floor of 450 Columbus Avenue, her cousin's family lived on the second floor, and good friends, the Gibsons, occupied the first floor. "We all grew up together as one big family," she said. "My parents moved from the South for work, but I've lived my whole life in the neighborhood. I attended the Charles

P. Perkins School that is condominiums now on St. Botolph Street and then I went to Jeremiah Burke High School in Dorchester." Her father had a day job with the Greyhound Bus Company but was a musician the rest of the time. In fact, he was the representative for the local Black Musicians Union and used to play with both downtown and out-of town-bands. Winnie remembers one time watching Lionel Hampton arrive at the Hi Hat while she and friends were outside watching people go into the club. "We weren't sure it was him and then he gave that wide smile and started unpacking his vibes and we knew. No one smiled like Lionel Hampton!"

When Winnie finished high school she worked for a while at the South End Neighborhood Action Project (SNAP), a local human-services organization that is now part of the city-wide Action for Boston City-Wide Development (ABCD.) She was planning to be a teacher, she said. "I knew I wasn't going to be a good wife and I certainly didn't want to be a *be all* to a man. In those days you were either going to be a teacher or a nurse if you didn't marry, and I thought I'd like to teach."

She started school at Boston State College for her training but when she got an offer to work as a customer services representative for New England Telephone Company with a much higher salary than SNAP could offer, she took it. "I thought I would be working just to pay for school, but it turned out to be a decision that would change my life forever." She stayed at New England Telephone as it became NYNEX, Bell Atlantic, and finally, Verizon. By the end of her career she was the manager of transportation for the company, overseeing the coordination, staffing, and maintenance for all the company's Boston-area trucks and truck drivers.

"It was difficult in a way because all of us were always on edge about keeping our jobs. Things were constantly changing and we had to keep learning new laws, new terminology, new technologies. I kept saying to my crew that we had to focus on doing our job better than anyone else so the company, whichever one was the owner at the time, doesn't decide to outsource our operations," Winnie said.

The "we" she was talking about included herself, a black woman, and forty white truck drivers. "It was unusual, I guess, for the times. You wouldn't find a black woman in charge of a crew of all white Caucasian men very often. They hazed me at first. But gradually they accepted me." Listening to her talk about her work and observing her genial manner, I had no doubt the men both respected and liked Winnie a great deal. "Some of the men were very caring and easy. Some of them wanted to be a pain, but it worked out. They came around eventually."

Winnie was retired when we spoke so I asked her how she filled her days. She said she grew up in the Union United Methodist Church on Columbus Avenue and was still very active there. Being part of the Sunday school, junior choir, and an usher, the church had been her mainstay as has been the Harriet Tubman House where she sings in the Platinum Chorus. Otherwise, she does the usual rounds of neighborhood places: the bank, the library, Lord & Taylor, Walgreens, Legal Sea Foods, the candy shop in the Prudential (a favorite), and local markets. Some days, when she goes to the Harriet Tubman House, she plays "a few games of Scrabble after lunch."

Though Winnie clearly had a fondness for the neighborhood, she was far from indifferent to its changing character—and far from content with it. On the contrary, she spoke openly about her disappointments. "I feel resentful," she said, "that I am often made to feel invisible. Maybe it's generational. I hope it's generational and it will pass, but there are very few places where I am made to feel part of this community. When I grew up—when I came of age—we were all about rights and about avoiding war. I don't know what values the young people have today."

Winnie said she was part of a group of about thirty in high school who fought for black studies. The head of the school was "reluctant to make a change. It was like pulling teeth to get him to agree. The attitude in those days was for authorities to think they might *let* you or *allow* you to do things, but we had to show them we demanded change and would not wait for their permission. We were determined and committed. I know there has to be a redeeming factor in this next generation. I'm not in the company of younger people a lot these days, but I just don't know." She ended with a sigh, looking off through the windows onto Columbus Avenue and the passersby.

POSTSCRIPT

I was planning to do my customary follow-up interview with Winnie a few months later, but when I called her to set a time, she said she was not well and would have to meet with me later. I was never able to reach her after that. Then, in January, 2014, the Union United Methodist Church secretary, Sybil Gilcrest, called me to say that Winifred Lowery had passed away the month before. I thought about her decision to stay single, and her ability to stand up for herself and her fellow black Americans. I admired her, and felt the loss of not knowing more.

—— • ——

Kathe McKenna, like Elna and Victor, moved to the South End as an adult with a plan to stay, but Kathe was different; she came with a mission. Grounded by a strong Christian faith, Kathe came to the neighborhood in the 1970s to serve the homeless and those in need. The South End had a countless number of people living at or well below the poverty level and she felt it would be a good place to work. Now, five decades later, she has become almost a legend for her dedication to serving poor people in this area of the city.

Kathe McKenna

Of all the South End lives I learned about during the period of these interviews, I found none so remarkable in its mix of simplicity and extreme complexity as Kathe McKenna's. Here was someone who had kept to a single vision for her life even though, over the years, she had been a devout Catholic, an associate of political radicals, founder and sustainer of a soup kitchen and service agency, a mother of four children, an advocate and developer of affordable housing, and a practicing Buddhist. She'd done it all. It should have been no surprise, then, when we sat down to talk, that it was hard to get her to focus on herself. She was constantly bringing in the names of other people who had helped in her efforts.

Perhaps the best place to begin Kathe's story is with her attendance at the Tennessee-to-Mississippi March Against Fear in 1966, when James Meredith, the civil rights activist and first African American to attend University of Mississippi, was shot, causing the march to catapult into a major protest with

15,000 participants. Kathe and her husband, John, had borrowed his parents' car for their honeymoon, but instead they used the car to drive south and join the march. Kathe identifies the aftermath of the march as the time she became radicalized.

Still, she confessed, much of her early commitment was probably rooted in family history. Her grandparents on her father's side had emigrated from Ireland, ending up in New York's Hell's Kitchen, and her mother's family was poor as well. By the time Kathe's parents met and married, however, both were thoroughly Americanized, living in a suburb of New York. Everyone on both sides were practicing Catholics.

Kathe went to public schools in Garden City, New Jersey, and attended the College of New Rochelle, where she majored in art. But these were the 1960s, and as Bob Dylan would remind everyone, "The times they are a-changing." Her art studies didn't stick. She soon turned to politics, becoming involved with a group at the college called Young Christian Students (YCS) whose mission was to get students involved in activities that advanced the teachings of the Gospels. When she graduated in 1964 she joined the YCS national staff in Chicago, traveling in the South and Northeast for the organization. Eventually ending up in Boston, she met people who were part of the Catholic Workers movement, a much more confrontational albeit still non-violent organization. It was while mimeographing leaflets at a Catholic Workers Newman Center that she met John McKenna.

John was teaching at Newman Preparatory School and, in keeping with Catholic Workers practice, shared his apartment with homeless men he met on the streets. Kathe, increasingly frustrated with mere organizing activities, was eager to do something similar. Besides, John had been on the 1965 Selma March for Civil Rights, as Kathe had been. Within a month of meeting, they were married.

Tremont Street was flooded with homeless men in those days, most of them with serious drinking problems. Kathe and John had taken an apartment on the South End's Upton Street with a plan to provide shelter for these men. But no one came. People were suspicious of the couple and their guileless hospitality until one winter night, when John found a man unconscious in a snowdrift and carried him home. When the man woke up, John and Kathe gave him breakfast and told him he could return the next night. The word was out. Their lifelong work had begun.

The couple maintained the Upton Street apartment, providing sleeping quarters and three meals a day for homeless and indigent men until Hope House, another halfway house in Boston, purchased it. Once the deal was closed, the McKennas approached Bob Bennett at Betty Gibson Real Estate to conduct a search for a new place to live and work. Like many other realtors at the time, Bob did not want to encourage homelessness in the neighborhood, but his mother knew of the McKennas from a priest friend, and she persuaded her son to help.

Bob showed Kathe and John a couple of buildings that the Boston Redevelopment Authority had slated for demolition and they eventually chose a building on Dartmouth Street with four apartments upstairs and three storefronts along the street. Naming it Haley House after a deceased colleague, they began operating as a soup kitchen, the cooking done upstairs and the serving on the street floor. "We were open 7:00 a.m. to 9:00 p.m. with me and volunteers doing most of the cooking. We lived in Haley House until our second daughter was born," Kathe said.

While they had both been involved in the civil rights movement in the 1960s, they, like many other activists, shifted their focus in the 1970s to demonstrate against the Vietnam War. John applied for status as a conscientious objector but both he and Kathe felt they needed to take a more extreme stand. Inevitably they became involved with Boston's Black Panthers, a revolutionary group fighting against oppression of black people, and with New York's Weathermen, a radical leftist group advocating violence to take down the U.S. government. At one point they moved to Long Island for teaching jobs while they considered joining the Weathermen officially, but the school jobs didn't work out and they returned to Boston and Haley House. Soon after John took a job with the Massachusetts Bay Transit Authority (MBTA) to support their growing family and Kathe ran the Haley House Soup Kitchen for more than forty hours a week. In 1974 she opened an elders' meal program to help older people in the neighborhood who couldn't afford food after paying their weekly rent.

Later in the 1970s Kathe spearheaded the Haley House organization to provide low-income housing for people displaced by the developers who were buying and turning old rooming houses into apartments and condominiums. The organization eventually acquired properties on Columbus Avenue, Massachusetts Avenue, and four other sites. Then, in 1983, Haley House purchased Noonday Farm in central Massachusetts, enabling families to raise organic produce and providing summer work for unemployed guests of Haley House. This was a rough time with the crack epidemic hitting Boston, and Kathe saw that the men needed to get out of the city and do physical work. Out of the farm effort grew the Haley House Bakery program, where guests learned to bake and sell bread out of the Dartmouth Street storefront. This evolved into a full-fledged on-the-job food preparation training program in Dudley Square.

I asked Kathe about John, since he had been involved in the early years of Haley House but didn't seem to be later on. She said he always took on the responsibility of supporting the family, and after teaching and a multitude of part-time jobs (including grave digging), he got the MBTA job as a security officer. It was while he was there that he went to law school and became a prosecutor for the MBTA, and later a judge for the Workers' Compensation Board. He was greatly disappointed when he was not rehired after fourteen years in the position, but greater hardship was to follow. When John was a student at Holy Cross College, he had played rugby. Later he was the captain of the Boston Rugby Team. So many blows to the head began to affect him around the age of sixty and eventually he couldn't do legal work. His last job was running the shower room at the Pine Street Inn, something he did faithfully until he could no longer work at all. He passed away in 2015.

As I listened to Kathe talk about her many years at Haley House, I wondered how she had the patience and steadfastness to work with some of the most disadvantaged people in our society, impoverished people who had lived on the streets for years. She said, "It's not work for the faint of heart, I admit. And in the early days, I was just an angry young woman wanting to change the world. But even early on, in my Catholic days, I was drawn to spiritual or mystical people. Tibetan Buddhism is a practice that provides the tools to end suffering—to understand the workings of your mind in order to deepen your peace of mind, compassion for others, and love. I have become grounded in that practice." She had recently returned from a hundred-day Tibetan Buddhist retreat outside Austin, Texas, where she "kept silence" for the entire stay. The goal of the retreat was "to help people become more fully compassionate while being present in the world," Kathe said. Deepening her work with the South Enders was what she had in mind.

— • —

I have placed Richard Pillard after Kathe McKenna because both have spent their professional lives in the South End caring for others. They are in the generation who came to the South End when it was still crime ridden with a conspicuous majority living at or below the poverty level. Kathe cared in one way, Richard in another. They both have had remarkable staying power in what could be considered very challenging careers. A factor was their attachment to the particular character of the neighborhood.

Richard Pillard

Richard Pillard moved to Cambridge in 1959 for a medical internship at Boston City Hospital, today's Boston Medical Center (BMC). He had graduated from the University of Rochester Medical School after turning down an offer from Harvard Medical School. It seemed a rather unusual decision, but when I asked him why he refused the offer that would make most med students envious, his first response was, "I was probably the lowest one on the acceptance list." I wasn't going to take this for an answer, so I asked him again why he had chosen Rochester. He had to talk about his background to explain.

Growing up in the small Ohio town of Yellow Springs, home to Antioch College, he escaped the mystique around Ivy League schools, he said. His parents both taught at Antioch and he ended up there himself. "I had been an undergraduate at Swarthmore, but transferred to Antioch because it had a co-op program where students worked and studied on alternate semesters. One of my co-op assignments was at New Jersey State Hospital, where I worked on a fifty-building campus that housed mentally ill patients. It wasn't easy work, but it was beguiling. My father was a dean at Antioch and did a lot of counseling to students whose stories I heard about—and that led me into medicine with a specialty in psychiatry. It was either a Ph.D. in clinical psychology or an M.D. in psychiatry. I chose the medical route," he said with the same matter-of-fact tone he had used when telling me about turning down Harvard Medical School. For his internship, he chose Boston City Hospital, which he liked for the comfortable commute from where he lived with his wife and daughters in Cambridge. Then how did he end up living in the South End? I asked.

"I didn't give much thought to the South End at the time. It seemed to me a dilapidated part of Boston with many people living in rooming houses or on the streets. There were abandoned buildings, some burned out, with broken concrete sidewalks and people sleeping in doorways—dereliction everywhere. Still, there was a stealthy charm about the South End—the rhythm of the bowfronts, the strict order of the Federal fronts still showing through in the 1960s even though much was in tatters. As it turned out, two women friends took a sick friend of theirs to the hospital. After I admitted him for treatment, we went back to their apartment on Gray Street. The brick buildings and dimly lit streets were like something from Sherlock Holmes and I told myself, 'Hey, I could actually live here.' My marriage was coming apart so I sold my Porsche sports car for $2,000, made a down payment on a Bond Street house, and moved to the South End. This was a Lebanese area with small stores and restaurants, some of which have remained relatively unchanged as the neighborhood has been gentrified. Once I moved in, I never wanted to leave."

Returning to the narrative of his career, Richard said after he finished his internship at BMC, he took up a psychiatric residency at Boston State Hospital in Mattapan, which was an entirely different story. "When I got to Boston State there were 1,800 patients, already down from 2,200. This was part of the *de-institutionalization* of mental health—an effort to have community health services that were smaller and located in neighborhoods where family and friends lived nearby." The Solomon Carter Fuller facility on Harrison Avenue, where Richard would eventually be medical director from 1985 to 1993, was part of this movement, as was the increased number of halfway houses and other community-based residences around lower Massachusetts Avenue.

The biggest shift in mental health treatment during the 1960s and 1970s, however, was the development of psychiatric medications. Richard and others of his era had been trained in the psychoanalytic approaches to mental health, but new drugs were coming along that could be far more effective for many conditions, especially the more serious ones. "I remember when I made the shift myself," Richard said. "I had been seeing a very depressed woman for months and months, treating her with psychotherapy. She never smiled once and she never felt good about anything. Then, one time, after I hadn't seen her for a couple of weeks, she came into my office all smiles—a completely different person. I presumed that an experience she had during our therapy produced the break-through, so I asked her. 'No,' she said. 'I think it was those pills you gave me two weeks ago.' I had completely forgotten that, rather in desperation, I had decided on a trial of Imip-ramine, an antidepressant just coming into use at the time. It was a turning point for me. I realized the power of medi-cation. Chronically depressed people are now mostly treated with medication as well as therapy."

For the last years before his retirement, Richard worked mostly with heroin addicts. "Doctors are under pressure these days to pay attention to relieving pain," he said. "People with severe anxiety as well as chronic pain are often given drugs like Percocet and Oxycontin, even though research shows these are often not the best treatment. Users can be at risk of becoming drug dependent, eventually seeking out heroin, which is easy to get and less expensive. We can treat opiate-dependent people with medications like methadone and sub-oxone that eliminate the craving, but the hard part is keeping people on their medication. Many opiate-dependent patients have panic attacks and end up using opiates as a form of self-medication."

We would return to panic attacks later, but I shifted from talk of his career to ask Richard about his personal life and inter-ests. He said that while he was in his residency before moving to the South End, he had undergone psychoanalysis and in the process discovered he was gay. His wife, Cornelia Livingston

Cromwell, from two distinguished Hudson Valley families, agreed they should end the marriage. "We have remained good friends and I am close to my daughters," he said. One of those daughters is a pediatrician, one a judge on the U.S. Court of Appeals in Washington, D.C., and one a social worker with a focus on psychiatric disorders among children.

Richard was eighty-one and retired when we met so I asked him how he was spending his time these days. "I am always in touch with my daughters," he said, "and I go to Vermont a lot to keep my eye on a summer home that's been in the family since I was a boy." But he will be studying the causes of panic attacks as well.

"Nobody knows the causes," he told me. "They come out of the blue, can go away, but then come back again. They cause an agoraphobic phenomenon (fear of the market place) where the victim doesn't want to go out. People who get attacks often get someone else to buy their groceries so they literally never leave their homes." He will look at the extensive literature available on the topic, then try to discover if there is an inherited tendency in panic anxiety that could lead to PTSD and/or drug addiction. Having spent so much time with people in the South End suffering from these afflictions, he wanted continue to try to find ways to treat them.

— • —

It was fairly easy to find older South Enders who had a few decades behind them to reflect on, but it was much harder to find young people who were willing to talk about the South End and their lives in the neighborhood. Fortunately Al Desta, the owner of the South End Food Emporium, met a young man in The South End Food Emporium who had read my history *A Block in Time* and told Al he loved to read history and knew quite a bit about the South End. Al passed Sebastian's name on to me. It turns out, Sebastian is not only a reader and good conversationalist but a writer of lyrics and poems, and a musician. Sebastian was happy to talk about what the South End was like in his youth, and how he views it now.

Sebastian Alonso

"Actually, it was safe on my block of Shawmut mostly because of Waltham Tavern. I grew up in the 1980s and 1990s across the street from it. The owners knew me. It was a tight community then, so I was okay. But we lived in the cross fire and there were gangs in those years. It was rough and just about impossible to avoid trouble if you were a kid my age," he said.

Sebastian Alonso said this about his early years on Shawmut Avenue: "My family didn't have much money. My parents slept in the living room of a tiny back apartment so me and my brother could have the bedroom. My father, a Cuban immigrant, worked as a day laborer on construction projects. My mother, from Lima, Peru, worked as a liaison to attorneys in a physical therapy office on Tremont. "They were typical of hundreds of immigrants who made the South End their first home in America, but this was decades after the great influx from Eastern Europe, Ireland, and the Middle East. Sebastian's family belonged to a more recent wave of newcomers.

"Actually, I had a great childhood," Sebastian said. "I remember me and my brother used to play a ball game that neighborhood kids made up where we threw a tennis ball against a neighbor's brick wall. We called it "outs." The lady who lived there was worried about her window so she finally kicked us out. But then we played the game in Hanson Street Park too. We even had what we thought looked like the Green Monster at Fenway Park. I played in two Little Leagues—Beacon Hill and South End. Our family outings were to go to Bob the Chef's on Sundays and sometimes, for a special treat, to the seafood restaurant called Porthole on Route One. My father loved it. We went to Beacon Hill, I remember, for trick-or-treating because the candy bars were bigger there."

An Asian man who never spoke used to bring the family fresh vegetables—probably from his garden, but they never really knew. There was a "kitty" store next to the bank where his mother got "seconds" or discounted goods: food, sheets, household things, games. She got bigger items like appliances and second-hand furniture from the Catholic social service agency, St. Vincent de Paul, on Washington Street. "I got my hair cut by an old pimp at Celebrity Barber," Sebastian recalled. "Lots of women were always in the shop. We didn't have it all, but we had Nintendo like other kids, and one summer, when I was twelve, me and my brother and a cousin did a program in South Boston called Artists for Humanity and I learned a lot. We had a topic and we tried ways to paint it. Mine was outer space."

I had to keep reminding myself that Sebastian was still

in his 20s. It seemed like he spoke of a neighborhood in the remote past, one that existed ages before the present boutiques, gourmet bakeries, and sidewalk cafes. But as recently as two decades ago, Sebastian's neighborhood still had pockets of first and second generations: Chinese and African Americans in the Castle Square area and Italian, Lebanese, and others further south. "Past Broadway," he said, "was all Irish."

The mix of people may have seemed safe and neighborly when he was going to the Josiah Quincy Elementary School and later to the Edwards Middle School in Charlestown, but when Sebastian got to South Boston High, he was away from his home turf and he started getting into trouble. "The Irish and the blacks stuck together, and the Latinos and Italians stuck together. I was friends with everyone, which was the big problem for me," he said. Eventually South Boston High kicked him out and he got sent to City on a Hill High School. "I was there two years but I got in trouble for fights there too, so they sent me to Boston High by the old Herald Building. By then I was into heavier crime and drugs like all my friends." He was able to graduate high school in 2004, but he and his friends were part of gang activities in Boston during those years. Many thought these activities had disappeared by the late 1990s but they hadn't. "Growing up in the South End, I was accustomed to death," he wrote in a short autobiography. "You grow immune to it like I was until 2013, when my close friend, an up-and-coming rapper named Ahmir, was killed on Boylston Street. Another childhood friend, Nicky, who goes by "Supreme," was arrested when he was completely innocent. I was there and I told the cops Supreme was not involved! He was black and they needed to make it look like a racial event. I even testified but they still sent him away."

I asked Sebastian what he and friends did when they hung out all day and what drew them into street life in the first place. He said he had a good family and his parents cared a lot about him and his brother. "I got some good old-fashioned beatings but my parents were always looking out for me. It had more to do with the neighborhood environment and the kids I made friends with. There was lots of cocaine on the streets in the 1990s. It was on every corner. There was pot everywhere, too. You didn't have to look for it. It looked for you. The South End was a 'filter' between Chinatown and Roxbury. The area around Tremont was heroin. Where I grew up, it was more crack. Albany Street was all pills. The streets were like a giant wave, and if you didn't know how to surf it you would get wiped out for good."

When he was around seventeen, Sebastian met the musician Square Root and got interested in making "music mixes on tapes." Then he tried stand-up comedy. "I was always into writing and friends told me I should try it. The first time, I killed it. It was great. So I did five shows after that and then one night I bombed so bad I had to quit. I had been watching people like Bernie Mac, Adam Sandler, and Eddie Murphy, and I thought I could do it, too. It didn't work out that way," he said, amused at himself.

When I asked Sebastian what he was doing for jobs during these years of "trying things," he named a few: the New

England Aquarium (in the whale watch booth), American Eagle at the Galleria Mall, the North End Mirabella Pool concessions stand, Emack & Bolio's Ice Cream, the Prudential Center Mall (selling soap at a stand), the Dimock Center (billing and computer data entry), Fire + Ice restaurant in Cambridge, On the Park restaurant, and more. He slowly worked himself up. Today is he a manger at Eddie Bauer.

When he was twenty-one, Sebastian fell in love with Vanessa, a girl around his age who lived in Jamaica Plain. "She was part Sicilian and part black and very beautiful. She had been an orphan but was adopted by a family that truly loved her. At one time, it was like in the movies and we were on call with each other all the time." The two took trips to New York, and they were getting along fine, but Sebastian went through some "rough patches," and the girl suddenly broke it off. "That was October 7, 2007, and I kept role-playing it over and over in my head. I cried a lot."

To console himself, Sebastian listened to singers like Frank Sinatra and Stevie Wonder, and especially *Since You're Gone* by Nolan Strong. He listened to that one hundreds of times and after a while he started thinking he could do this himself— that is, "get into music." In 2014 he formed a group called The Pheromones with a drummer, a bass player, a guitarist, and two female vocalists. They practice at the Harriet Tubman House on Columbus Avenue and Sebastian hopes to be performing onstage soon. And yes, he has met Brianna Hall, who has "more than replaced" Vanessa in his life.

When I asked to see something Sebastian had written, he

explained to me that he could never be sure whether to call something he wrote a poem or a song. He writes both but this one, he said, is a poem.

Shoulders Karma

My chin misses her shoulder
but her shoulder found a new chin
now resting over my Darling's shoulder.
How can I win?

How can I win love back from her shoulder
if love is over? I should begin
to find a new shoulder
that's a closer match for my chin.

It's not just her shoulder.
I also hope her lips never find
a kiss that enfolds her
as I once showed her, way back in time

So have fun with your shoulder
That's when I told her:
Keep this in mind:

When he says it's over
I'll have found a new shoulder
I can call mine.

After Sebastian and I had met for what I thought was the last time, he called me to say he wanted to talk again. He told me he was worried about something. When we met a week later, he said he wanted to be sure he gave me the right impression about his South End feelings. "I don't want you to think that because I talked about those hard times in the past that I am pleased with the present. If I could go back in the past and have the neighborhood the way it was then, I'd take it in a second." He said the hippies—meaning my generation in the 1970s and 80s—would say "hi" and people mixed. "Back then people didn't call your home a *unit*. The other day a guy brushed by me and didn't even look. Didn't say a word and he had bumped into me. It's all changed now."

— • —

Paul Duffy is a few decades older than Sebastian, but I couldn't help seeing similarities between the two. Both have a certain *joie de vivre* that an observer can't miss, and the South End suits both as backdrop for their energetic personalities. Neither would find an easy, comfortable place in the suburbs, I thought, or even in other parts of Boston, but the South End is perfect for them. Duffy, though not born in the neighborhood like Sebastian, could almost claim he was. He's active in the neighborhood and feels just as at home as Sebastian does.

Paul Duffy

The luck of the Irish is *bad* luck, but one South Ender, an Irishman to the core, seems to have had mostly *good* luck. At least that's the way Paul Duffy ("call me Duffy") of Clarendon Street sees it, which may be unavoidable in his case, viewing the glass, as he always does, as half full.

Here's what Duffy said about his Irish childhood: "I was the oldest of eight children. My mother and father were both Irish and all my grandparents were from Ireland—all devout Catholics." Duffy's father, who was called "Himself" by members of the family, including Himself, worked two jobs all his life to support the family. The family lived in a house on Roxbury's Fort Hill, where Duffy and all his siblings grew up. "My socks had holes in them and my mother bought work pants with tool hooks because they were the cheapest available. None of the other kids wore them and eventually I didn't either. I wanted to look good so I got myself a paper route with two hundred customers. Then I could buy my own socks and clothes. I did my own laundry, too, so my T-shirts would be really white."

A lot of the customers on that paper route were Jews on Blue Hill Avenue who often paid him in fruits and vegetables. It wasn't what he had in mind, but when he took them home, his mother told him they were worth more than money. "When do we get fruit and vegetables in this house?" she asked. He said it was a lesson about value that he never forgot.

He was resourceful when it came to schemes for getting by. For example, Duffy used to take newspapers down to the Combat Zone in Scully Square on a Saturday night and sell them to the men, especially the sailors. "I sold the *Record American,* which published the numbers people would be betting on. They'd buy the papers, check the numbers, and then put them down on the tables. After I sold a lot, I'd go back to the room behind the bar to watch shows with mostly music and dancing girls, and when everybody came back there later, I'd go to the front and pick up the papers and sell them at the next bar." I asked Duffy how old he was then and he said, "Oh, eleven, twelve, thirteen. I was out on my own by then."

He made it as far as the sixth grade without getting expelled, but the principal sent him to a special school after that. It was called a "vocational school" but he told me it was actually an extended detention. Nevertheless he ended up liking it, learning sheet metal welding, cooking, blacksmithing, woodworking, and other skills that would come in handy later. The program was supposed to end after a year but the superintendent was fond of Duffy and got him into English High. "It was because I looked like his son who had been killed in the war, I think, but I didn't last at English, not even to the end of tenth grade." Maybe it was just as well. An education would not be essential for him to get what he wanted.

Duffy's first real job was working at the Flower Exchange on Tremont Street when he was fourteen. It lasted until he was eighteen when he joined the Navy. Once out of the Navy in 1961, he began working in sales for Dynamo Industries—a job he thought would "make me lots of money." When his employers found out he had no real schooling past eighth grade, however, they demoted him to factory worker. "It wasn't long, though, before they saw what I could do and hired me back for sales, where I did make lots of money." Later, he began working for Street and Company, a real estate agency on Beacon Hill. While there, he told me, he learned of two buildings near the Flower Exchange that were going up for sale. Seizing the moment, he borrowed $2,000 from friends and family for a down payment and bought 57 Gray Street and 37/39 Clarendon Street in the South End.

By this time, Duffy had married a minister's daughter from South Carolina. The two of them were swept up by the 1960 wave of rebellion against conventional society. Their first adventure was to live in a teepee in Maine. The next was to travel abroad, starting in North Germany and going as far south as Morocco before looping back to England. With their travels over in 1971, the two moved into Duffy's place on Gray Street. His wife was teaching at the Boston University School of Social Work and Duffy was back at Street and Company in a managing job.

He had an experience while at Street and Company, he told me, that made him change his life. A woman whose Beacon Hill property he was maintaining called Duffy in to say she objected to someone he had assigned to her. When asked to give a reason, all she would say was she didn't want "those kind of people working there." The episode made Duffy so angry he quit Street and started his own company: O'Ryan, Lopez, and Chin Management and Maintenance in the South End. The names were made up, but his first employees included a Venezuelan, a Vietnamese, and an African American. Duffy is now retired, but is the company is still doing a good business.

Well, he's not exactly retired. In 2006, Duffy oversaw the re-development of his three houses on Gray and Clarendon. It took fourteen months, he told me, but when it was done the complex had six new apartments and 1,400 square feet of commercial space. He kept the entire top floor, accessible by private elevator, as his own apartment, replete with cherry paneling, working fireplace, deep leather chairs, and all the latest lighting fixtures and kitchen equipment. He is active in the Ellis Neighborhood Association, the Learning Project, the South End Business Alliance, and the Greater Boston Concierge Association, which keeps him busy visiting restaurants, galleries, and special events that concierges need to know about. Oh yes, and he regularly plays poker with his Ellis Neighborhood friends and with a handful of buddies who occupy those leather armchairs in his living room to drink bourbon and smoke cigars over more "casual" poker games.

When I first met with Duffy, he told me he was "a bit of a rogue." It came up again when he was describing how he was in school. Now in his seventies—jaunty mustache, fashionably trimmed beard, dapper shirts and pants—Duffy had clearly kept elements of that description. "I like flirting. I said I'm a rogue but I'm all talk. On the other hand, I am single, not ugly, I live in the South End, and have a little money. Besides, I like to look good and dress nice." Why wouldn't people, especially women, find him especially likable? He goes out four nights a week, he told me, usually to restaurants and cultural events in the South End.

— • —

Duffy and everyone profiled in this book so far have all lived in the South End for at least two decades. Not Chris Fagg, though she is one of the greatest enthusiasts of the neighborhood I met. She moved from Tennessee to the South End in 2010 and feels completely at home, declaring she will never leave. The neighborhood has welcomed her, she said, and she goes to the South End Library almost daily. I thought it said a lot about the neighborhood in its present era that she felt so immediately comfortable. Here's her story.

Chris Fagg

I had seen Chris Fagg at the South End Library when I went to pick up books. She was often outside in the park or talking to people at the desk inside. I noticed her for her friendly manner but also for her large body and the slightly balding spot in an otherwise full head of red hair. She was usually wearing a skirt, tights, and shoes with a low heel. After we were introduced and talked a while, I asked her if she'd tell me about her life and any thoughts she had about the South End. But first I asked what she'd like me to call her.

"Well, I like Chris," she said, "because it can be for a man or a woman. I'm transgender so I like that it's both." Chris is transitioning from a man to a woman and her surgery will occur sometime in 2016. "I have someone at Boston Medical Center who is my primary care physician with special training in gender issues. We meet every two months or so and he will be assisting the surgeon during the operation. When it's done, I'll be completely female."

This type of operation is no longer news, Chris and I agreed. Many, including famous people, have had sex changes and many more have talked openly about their gender identities. Times have changed, but I asked Chris if she felt she had been treated differently or discriminated against while growing up. "Well, I've never had anyone be really mean to me. It was just starting to be a real issue in college. I always knew I was different and that I felt like a woman inside, but I was always just me. I will be the same after the operation, I guess. I'm always just how I am."

Chris grew up on a farm in Tullahoma, Tennessee—the only town on Earth with that name, she told me. "It comes from the Sauk and Cherokee tribes of the 1600s and 1700s but it's just a normal town with three malls, a new strip mall along the highway that we don't need, a library, city hall, and churches on every corner—maybe forty of them! One thing is different, though: the town is surrounded by an Air Force base, with planes overhead all the time. My father worked on the base during World War II and lots of relatives did, too."

It was the farm, however, and not the town or base that dominated Chris's life. "It was a real working farm with hogs, chickens, ducks, cattle and a few crops—corn, beans, peppers, and watermelon mostly—and a farmhouse with a front porch. Not real big. My grandmother always said the house had ghosts—strange things like the shower coming on all of a sudden, or a door locked from the inside when nobody was there. Once my cousin and I were outside and ran in the house to shut the windows before a storm hit, but they were all closed. Things like that. Who knows? Anyway, we never really questioned her. My uncle and two aunts on my father's side were around our house a lot, especially my Aunt Cricket, and my cousins. The family goes back to the late 1600s. My father came from a family of nine children and my mother was one of eight. They dated fourteen years before they married but I guess everybody knew they always would. I was an only child but I had a twin sister who died at birth."

Growing up, Chris stayed mostly around her parents and extended family, but when she went to Franklin County High School, she "got more social," making friends mostly by playing on the baseball and football teams. After graduation she went on to Middle Tennessee State University on a sports scholarship, graduating with a major in history. "I was an average ball player and an average student but I volunteered for things and I read all the time. I always had my nose in a book." She worked in construction for a year after college, but eventually returned to the farm to help manage it. I asked if she thought of doing something else with her education but she said, "Well, my parents were getting older and they needed me. I suppose I might have become a lawyer. I have cousins in the Navy and we have three Navy lawyers in our family, but I stayed home to help."

After her parents died, however, Chris sold the farm and moved to Boston, joining a cousin to care for an elderly aunt. When that aunt died, Chris began working part-time as a personal care attendant for elderly and handicapped people. A couple of years ago she was diagnosed with Asperger's syndrome, but she never thought that was an accurate description. "I was different with people and my cousin made me see a doctor. I guess that's what they thought I had, but I'm just the way I am. I like people."

The last time we met, Chris talked mostly about the South End. She said she feels very much a part of the neighborhood and loves being able to walk to everything, especially the library and Trinity Church, the two places where she spends most of her time. She's on the altar guild and the flower guild and does the outreach program in the Copley Square area for the church. "We make sandwiches and take meals, gloves, scarves, whatever the homeless people in the area need. At first it was just me and one other person but now we have ten people who do it, which is really nice." She said she liked the "feeling of history in the South End and the people are friendly—the people and all their dogs!"

— • —

The Fantuzzis are newcomers like Chris, but they represent a wave of young families drawn to the South End for its tot lots, tree-lined parks, historic homes, and active, engaged residents. A couple of decades ago, young people had hesitations about raising children in the South End. No longer. The neighborhood is attractive, well maintained, and safe! The Fantuzzis chose their house on Pembroke Street with enthusiasm, and though they've only recently settled in, they're very much at home. Here's what they had to say about their lives and the neighborhood.

Graig And Jackie Fantuzzi

Graig and Jackie Fantuzzi bought their house on Pembroke Street in 2014, moving their family in while work was still being done on the house. When I asked Graig why they had chosen the South End, he said, "It has both indoor and outdoor space, and it feels like a real neighborhood. Besides, it's great to have more parking space, which we didn't have where we lived before. It's great, too, that we've been able to meet our neighbors easily and quickly." In the warmer months, Jackie said, they even had an occasion to join the old South End tradition of stoop-sitting.

"Our experience has been like a spider-web," Graig explained, "with connections going in all directions. We got to know two families with children early on, but we've met neighbors through the Pilot Block Neighborhood Association, United South End Settlements, and just meeting dog walkers and people on the street. And like most people who choose to live here," Graig added, "we like the diversity of the South End, a welcome change from some of the previous places we've lived."

When I asked about those places, Graig said, "We were in a much more settled and even closed community in New York. I worked on Wall Street, trading on the bond market from 1998 to 2007. Almost all our friends were in the same line of work and same social circle. We had jobs in the city and the places we lived were similar. When we came to Boston, we lived on Beacon Hill, which we liked, but there are strong traditional ties there that can make you feel closed off from people who have lived there a long time. Besides, many of the young families we got to know there were moving out for more space."

Graig and Jackie both grew up in Toms River, New Jersey, though in different sections of the town. Graig's father was a college baseball coach, his mother a school librarian and teacher. While Graig was quarterback on the high school football team and involved in many activities ("and known by everyone!" Jackie said), he was a also serious student, graduating as valedictorian of his class. While he had other choices for college, he said, he chose Washington and Lee where he graduated in 1996—once again, class valedictorian. Receiving a Fulbright to Singapore after graduation probably shaped his future career more than anything. "I was a kid who never had a passport, and suddenly I was going to Singapore to research major financial institutions. These were the booming years of the 1990s so I had a unique opportunity."

Once back in the U.S. he took a job with Morgan Stanley,

where he worked for ten years as a strategist for bond market investors. That job gave him and Jackie, married by then, the chance to live in Japan for a year and a half. "I have been very fortunate. I was good at my job but I was in an industry that was growing. The Fulbright gave me connections at a good time, and I was able to use my training. A lot of people can do this kind of work, but I happened to be at the right place at the right time." It was typical of his modesty.

Jackie's father, one of six children, was from an Irish-English family. After high school he joined the Air Force, where he served in Japan during the Vietnam War. While stationed there, he met a Japanese woman in a Hakata bowling alley and within a year the two were married. Jackie said her father's family disapproved of the match at first—her mother was a tomboy who rode a moped and was four years older than her father—but the big objection was to her being Japanese. Eventually she won everyone over, Jackie said.

After high school, Jackie went to Rutgers University, where she got both a B.S. and later an M.S. in animal science. Her real love had always been animals and she had considered veterinary school, but was eager to start working. The best option at the time was a job in a pharmaceutical lab but she quickly realized the work wasn't for her. Eventually she went back to school for an M.A. in animal psychology, but by then she and Graig were already planning their move to Boston so she never entered the field. It's still her dream to set up a consulting business for owners of pets with behavioral problems.

Jackie and Graig knew each other in high school but never

dated. Then when Graig returned from the Fulbright in Singapore they ran into each other at a local hangout in Toms River. Both remembered that back when they were seniors, Graig had written a note by Jackie's picture in her high school yearbook. It said, "To my future wife." They said it was uncanny since fifteen years later, they got married.

Now, as part of the South End, the Fantuzzis are throwing themselves into neighborhood life. I first met them on Halloween when everyone in the family, including their two little boys, was dressed up as characters from *Charlie and the Chocolate Factory* (green hair and all) to trick-or-treat with other parents and grandparents from Pilot Block. Halloween was barely celebrated in the South End in the 1970s and early 1980s when my children were little, but since then it has become a festive, high-profile holiday with hundreds of kids from all over the South End on the streets in costumes. The Fantuzzis had a party in their kitchen after the trick-or-treaters had gone to bed for families who had survived the onslaught.

On a spring morning a few months after we met, I was walking to the Southwest Corridor Park when I ran into Graig. He had a trash-picking tool in one hand and a plastic bag in the other. "Helping clean up the street," he said. He was already in the tradition of many South Enders who have taken it upon themselves to try to make the neighborhood a more pleasant place to live.

— • —

Mary Gillis lives on Upton Street, only a few blocks from the Fantuzzis and almost around the corner from Sebastian, but her world rarely, if ever, intersects with either Jackie's or Graig's. Nevertheless, the South End has been central to her life and work. Mary is a fabric artist, and while she came to the neighborhood when she and her husband bought an Upton Street rooming house in 1972, she became its sole owner in the 1990s and renovated it to perfectly accommodate her life as an artist. Today, with a studio on the top floor of her house and fellow artists on nearby streets and avenues, she has made the South End her home and workplace.

Mary Gillis

When Mary and Charlie Gillis bought the house on Upton Street, it was a licensed lodging house with seven tenants, each renting a room and sharing the one bath. The lodgers paid rent by the week—$8 or $12 depending on room size. One of the Upton Street tenants was an elderly veteran of World War I who stayed until he died at the age of ninety-four. While a few were eccentric and had problems, for the most part Mary said she found running the rooming house interesting and rewarding. When the city built a number of subsidized apartments in the 1980s, however, local coffee shops, restaurants, and non-profits that served the lodging house clientele closed, and the demand for rooms disappeared. Mary said the experience of being in charge of a rooming house and dealing with tenants whose lives were very different from her own helped her as much as her formal education to get along with all kinds of people and to welcome adventure.

Mary grew up in Roslindale, Massachusetts, attending

Catholic schools through grade twelve. Recalling her child-hood, she mentioned two particular incidents. Her mother, she said, would constantly send her back upstairs in the morning to change her clothes for school because Mary mixed colors, prints, and plaids—something that was not "acceptable" in the those days. Second, she took a class at the local Singer machine shop at age twelve and learned to sew. She made her first simple jumper in that Singer class and never quit sewing after that. In fact, she made most of her clothes as she grew up—even through her college years at Northeastern University and graduate school at Bentley University.

In the mid-1970s, Mary visited a Provincetown craft gallery with a beautiful handmade Amish quilt on display. She was smitten. It cost a lot more than she could afford, she said, but she took long minutes to study it. Soon after, she got a book from the library on basic quilt-making and made a doll's quilt for her friend's daughter. It was the beginning. She was working at an accounting job and running the rooming house, but the love of quilting took hold.

Then, in the early 1990s, Mary took a class with an artist where, for the first time, she learned color theory and design as applied to textiles. In 1999 she renovated the Upton Street house to make a triplex rental unit on the lower three floors and a duplex for herself on the top two. The lower of her two floors became a modern kitchen adjacent to formal dining and living rooms, the top floor became a bedroom and large sunny studio with cutting table, sewing and supply tables, and floor-to-ceiling shelves holding hundreds of fabrics all organized by color families: blues from midnight to powder; oranges from coral to dark burnt sienna; reds from pink to scarlet; and on and on. A few fabrics are solid in color, but most are prints with patterns far exceeding the common stripes, plaids, or polka dots: flowers, insects, umbrellas, cars, fish, cats, space ships and nameless abstract designs. Altogether, the fabrics represent about twenty years of collecting. Given her childhood mixing and mismatching outfits, Mary thinks being a quilt artist was her destiny.

Mary's repertoire is no longer limited to quilting; now her handwork includes wall hangings and fabric collages. Her "Missiles and Oil Wells" banner has been shown in juried shows across the country and was brought to Washington, D.C., for a peace march in 2005. Her "Float Like a Butterfly, Sting Like a Bee" banner, celebrating Muhammad Ali, the great heavyweight champion and draft-refuser, is hanging in a hospice chapel at Louisiana State Penitentiary at Angola. She has recently finished a wall hanging laser-printed with the names of all 4,486 American soldiers killed in the Iraq war.

It would seem a woman who has run a rooming house, worked as an accountant and makes fabric art might be a quiet and retiring person. Quite the contrary: Mary is a hiker and adventurer. The year she graduated from college she and three friends drove across the country, camping all the way. When they got to the Rocky Mountains she told me, "I would have been happy if they had just left me there. I loved the mountains and I always will. I went to Nepal and have been to northern India seven times to hike in the mountains there."

She has also done the two-hundred-mile coast-to-coast walk across the narrow part of northern England, and numerous other hikes in the English countryside where one "still has to clamber over old-fashioned stiles."

Where did such an attachment to mountains come from, I wondered, given she had spent her life in eastern Massachusetts. "I didn't make the connection until one day I was talking with my mother-in-law about our shared love of the book *Heidi*. I read the book when I first learned to read, and images of the little girl in the Swiss Alps with her grandfather made a strong impression on me." Before I left her house where she would be spending hours hand stitching and periodically working on taxes for clients that day, I asked if there was anything else engaging her these days. I wasn't surprised at the answer. "Well, yes," she said, "I've made a wall hanging and an artist book based on themes of *Moby Dick,* which I love. I'm taking a course on bookmaking right now. I'm interested in doing more books."

—·—

At the opposite end of the South End from Mary's house is the apartment of another artist who also works with textiles but in a totally different way. Tom Stocker makes paintings of wool, cotton, and silk rugs. I first saw these exquisite replicas when I went on a South End Open Studios tour in 2013. As soon as I entered his studio and saw the array of detailed paintings of Oriental, tribal, and modern rugs, I wanted to know what started Tom off in the direction he took as an artist, and how he connected to other South End artists as well. His story gave me answers to both.

Tom Stocker

Tom Stocker's living room windows—a phalanx of glass from floor to ceiling—open onto a cityscape of church spires, shining copper gutters, blacktop roofs, the Hancock's knife-sharp corners, the Cyclorama's dome, and a hodgepodge of curved windows, brick surfaces, and mansard slate roofs. While the apartment that offers this view is on Northampton Street, just over the edge of what is commonly thought of as the South End, Tom points out that the view essentially encompasses the entire neighborhood. It was a late summer afternoon when I visited with the light painting everything in shades of dusty rose. I'm not surprised Tom chose to leave his 1,680-square-foot apartment of thirty-nine years on Gray Street to live in an apartment with only 850 square feet of indoor space. The deck takes in more than a square mile through the windows.

I immediately asked Tom about the paintings and how he happened to focus almost exclusively on rugs as his subject.

He began by describing an early interest in "floor cloths"—canvas-mat paintings that the British made in the eighteenth century and which the colonists, as early as 1760s, were producing as well. Using stencils or painting freehand, artists created floor cloths for some of the finest homes in early America, including the White House when it was occupied by John Adams and Thomas Jefferson.

Tom's early attraction to painting began with his boyhood in Methuen, Massachusetts. It was an unusually pretty town, mostly because three very wealthy businessmen had tried to outdo each other in making the city attractive. Tom lived in Methuen until he was fourteen and its exceptional beauty had left a strong impression.

What else, I asked. "Well, my mother loved the movies and she would travel all the way to Lawrence, sometimes three times a week, to see double features in various movie theatres there. I went with her from when I was very little and I still remember those times. She was a very romantic, dreamy, distant kind of person and movies were her obsession. She knew all the stories, all the actors, everything about everyone she had watched. Once, I remember, in 1953 we walked two and a half miles in the snow to see *Quo Vadis* because it was only showing one time and there would be no transportation during the storm. I was often late for school or missed school altogether because of the movies. When my mother was ill and dying, I told her I remembered seeing my first movie, *The Red Shoes*, when I was four years old. 'Oh no,' she quickly corrected me. 'There were many others before that.' "

The most important influence on Tom's future career as an artist was probably his maternal grandfather, Tom said. That grandfather had been a manager in a textile mill and, over the years, had collected thousands of discarded fabric scraps left on the mill floors. When he retired, his grandfather began braiding these scraps, over time making hundreds of rugs. "These were not ordinary braided rugs," Tom said. "They were among the finest people had ever seen. He dyed some of the fabrics to get the colors just right. I would watch him by the hour. We were not allowed to talk while he worked. I'd be there with my sister and cousins and we'd be watching him. After a while, I'd look around and all the others would be gone and it would be just me with my grandfather."

His grandfather died when Tom was nine, around the same time his parents separated. His mother, a French Canadian Catholic, and his father, an English Protestant policeman, had a difficult marriage, and when they split his mother decided immediately to move to Monterey, California, taking Tom and his sister with her. The venture didn't last long, however, and when they returned east, his mother got an apartment in Lawrence, where Tom went to high school.

"It was a tough school in those days. The kids were tough. The girls hid razor blades in their beehive hairdos; the boys were threatening. The irony was, we had to wear suit coats and ties and address our teachers as master and miss. It was a huge school. I was in the college track so I wasn't really part of the rough crowd. I survived."

Tom had planned to go to college after high school

graduation, but that year his father died and life changed radically without his support. On the advice of a brother-in-law in the Army Language School in Monterey, Tom decided to join the Air Force, hoping to get into a language school with that branch of the service. Happily, he qualified for its Russian program at Indiana University and immediately enlisted. Then life changed again, this time beginning "a period of trouble and turmoil," he said.

At Indiana University, fellow airmen pressured Tom to double date, which he didn't want to do. When he finally confessed to a woman friend that he was gay (though the word wasn't in use at the time), she thought he "needed help" and reported him to his officers. It turned out to be a nightmare, resulting in his discharge in 1962. In order to change that ruling from an "undesirable" to "general" discharge, he had to undergo two years of therapy, after which he had to secure letters from a priest, a professor, and a therapist saying he was "cured. " With those letters he could go before a Review Board in Washington where the "brass" could then give him a general discharge. "It was strange," Tom said, "because clearly they knew exactly the situation, but avoided any questions relating to my supposed cure. They had been through this whole sham performance many times before and knew they had to play their part. That was the 60s, and it was all going to change soon, but that was too late to affect me."

After the Air Force ordeal, Tom moved back home to Boston where he got his B.A. in Russian at the University of Massachusetts, Boston. For a while he drove a taxicab, for a while he had an antiques shop in the South End, and for a while he tried real estate. "I got my real estate license, but I hated it. It was the early 1980s and people didn't have money to buy homes. We were selling to the bottom feeders and they were pushing to get bargains. I ended up managing apartments and I couldn't stand that either." Finally, around 1990, he started painting full time. "At that point I said I was going to paint or starve."

The first rug painting Tom ever sold was purchased by a curator at Fidelity Investments to hang in the hallway outside the CEO's office. When the CEO saw it, however, he asked what they had spent—and bought the piece for himself. Then the same buyer commissioned Tom to paint a nine-foot depiction of an Oriental rug for the lobby of the Fidelity headquarters in downtown Boston. Since then Tom's rug paintings have been hung in institutions and galleries in Boston and New York and he has settled into a studio at 450 Harrison Avenue, a building with sixty tenants in the new South of Washington Artist (SOWA) Guild. The building has open studios every first Friday of the month, Tom said, and you never know who will come by. "Once a group of Arabs drifted through my studio and returned later, eventually buying three paintings for a total of $20,000."

At the end of our conversation, Tom reflected on his childhood and life in a way he had not before. He said that even though he had lived through the strife with his parents, been a latchkey kid, and moved from place to place, not to mention the painful Air Force experience, it had all "enriched my life and made me what I am today." Not forgetting the support and encouragement from his partner Jim Alexander and fellow artists in the South End, he added, "I am fortunate to have earned recognition from others of my success. It is the difficult things that produce the greatest benefits."

— • —

Tom Stocker had his roots in small-town Massachusetts. Tei-riera Putman's are in the deep South. Tom is an artist, Teri is a child-care professional. Their lives are a study in contrast in terms of their families, interests, and ambitions. But I found a common thread in their stories. While both have had to endure hard experiences that could have prevented them from future success, both achieved their goals and came to a deeper understanding of their real values. Both are examples of how one can survive hardship and prevail.

I knew Teri when she was a teenager on Holyoke Street in the late 1970s, but as the years went by, I rarely saw her. Her mother had moved away and I thought she probably had as well. Then around 2005 I began seeing her on Columbus Avenue often—so often that we got reacquainted one day when this project was getting underway. I asked her if we could talk further and she graciously agreed.

Teiriera Putman

Teiriera (Teri) Putman told me she is in the middle of five generations of people who have meant the most to her: her two grandmothers, her mother, her three daughters, and now her four grandchildren. "I have been shaped by my family," she said, and as she talked about the events of her life, her work, and the South End, she kept returning to this theme.

It was true that her family had lived on Holyoke Street for many years, but when her aunt who had owned the house died, the family moved into the Methunion Manor. Since then she had gone to school, had a family, and recently opened a new business, Families First Day Care Center, on Columbus Avenue between Braddock Park and West Newton Street.

"I have been in day care for young children for nineteen years," she said. "When I opened Families First in 2007, I went from ten children in my home to fifty children in the center." It was a big jump, but with so many schools, hospitals, Boylston Street shops, and businesses in the area, there was a need and she wanted to address it. Children came from all over Boston, some on the state's Child Care Choices voucher system, some paying the full tuition. They represented the whole range of ethnic backgrounds.

Teri came to her understanding of children and families gradually. Growing up in a large family, she only slowly realized what had been the formative experiences of her life. It was a long story, she said, beginning with her two grandmothers, especially one of them. "My grandmother on my father's side was a model for me and I've always thought I took after her in many ways. That grandmother owned her own farm, a rare circumstance for a black woman in Georgia. My great grandfather was a slave owner but he wanted to be sure his out-of-wedlock daughter would be taken care of. My grandmother was very fair-skinned and even passed for a white person, but she married a black man and stayed in the black culture, raising thirteen children while running an open and welcoming household for everyone around." Teri loved to visit her.

"When my father was killed in an automobile accident on a Georgia back road, I was at my grandmother's house. I watched her face when my father's cousin, who was responsible for the accident, came to tell her the awful news. My grandmother stayed very composed and listened while the cousin told her what happened. I can remember it to this day. She had a lot of strength," Teri said.

Soon after the accident, Teri's mother, Margaret Putman, moved north to Boston's South End where Teri's aunt,

Beatrice Moon, lived. By then, Margaret had two children and was pregnant with a third. "I didn't really know what the move was all about when it happened. I didn't know that it was going to be a permanent move, so it took me a while to realize it was. My aunt had children and we lived in her house so I just started playing with my cousins and got used to it."

In the 1950s the South End was "wall to wall kids," Teri said. "I remember the South End as a world full of playmates—children everywhere, all day long. It was the city, and there were always things to do. We never went anywhere alone, we were always in groups, boys and girls. As girls we played Red Rover, Chinese jump rope, Double Dutch, and Head of the Class, and we hung around the neighborhood together. When we got a little older we went bowling at a popular alley on Huntington or to the movies. We could go to a cartoon and double feature for fifty cents—and there were movie theaters everywhere!"

But Teri said her girlhood was also difficult. When she was nine years old, she started crying a lot. She wasn't sure why but thought it might be because she was finally feeling the loss of her father. She had been close to him and had memories of him giving her treats—once, a silver dollar. The crying began to subside, she said, but as a teen she started to have strange compulsions. She felt like she couldn't get clean. She wanted to wash all the time. She also started having migraines that became so severe her mother took her to a doctor to see if it was a brain tumor. She was fourteen at the time.

The story of Teri's discovery and recovery from blurred

memories is a moving and heroic one. Although she graduated from Roxbury High in 1973, had a child, went to work (first at the Prudential and then in child care programs), and got an associate's degree in Early Childhood Education at Wheelock College, she still struggled with something she couldn't quite identify. Finally, in consultations with a doctor at Whittier Street Health Center, conversations at church-group retreats, and by reading countless books on compulsive behavior, she uncovered memories of a maternal uncle's sexual abuse when she was a young child in Georgia. After a long and difficult struggle, she could finally acknowledge what had happened.

But that didn't mean everything was fine. "By then I was about thirty," Teri said. "I was angry and I couldn't concentrate and I knew I had to confront the uncle and tell him what he had done." When he came to visit her aunt and mother around that time, she finally did. "I told him I remembered it and how it had affected me all these years. I had to do it, and when it was over I felt a huge weight had been lifted from me." It took a while for her mother to accept what happened, but she finally did. "She finally let down, and things got easier."

Teri began caring for infants and toddlers in her home while taking classes in the field of early childhood development. Then, in the early 2000s, she started thinking about the vacated Videosmith storefront at 465 Columbus Avenue for a child-care center. She would get all the necessary licensing, develop the space, hire staff, and establish it as LLC with herself as owner. Since it would be a new facility for the neighborhood, I asked her what she noticed about the South End's child population today compared to what it was when she opened the Center.

"When I first started day care for infants," she said, "there weren't very many babies in the South End. Now it seems they are everywhere. Still, I think a lot of people move in the South End for a while, but as soon as they have children—especially more than one—they move out." She said she had seen changes among the children, too, especially an increased incidence of autism. "We can sometimes even catch it when the children are in the infant's room. It's something very new."

I asked Teri at the end of our interview if she minded me telling the story of her uncle's abuse and how she had struggled. "Oh no," she answered quickly, "I think it can help other people when they know what you have been through and survived." She went on to say she had always thought of herself as a strong person. When I followed up by asking her why, she said, "Well, I think it goes back to watching my grandmother. I admired how she was, and it made me want to be strong, too."

— • —

After a few interviews, I began to notice how many South Enders I spoke to had started their own businesses. Teri had begun hers, and there were two others I would talk to as well. It made me wonder if this was coincidental or if it had to do with the layout of this section of the city—main streets with commercial properties and small high-density residential blocks in between. I wondered if there would be the same percentage of adventuresome people among residents in Medford or Weston, for example. I couldn't be sure. Certainly with the internet making it so easy, there were more people working in their own homes, but that's not the same as opening a shop on the street and attracting customers. The next few interviews seemed to indicate the character of the neighborhood had something to do with it.

Henry Wong was a co-owner of a high-fashion boutique on Tremont Street when I met him. He was a classic South End entrepreneur, though his life took a few turns before he became one.

Henry Wong

Henry Wong can remember his grandfather who came from Canton (now Guangzhou), China, to the United States to work on the railroads. At one point that grandfather went back to Canton to find a bride and brought her to settle with him in Evanston, Wyoming, population 5,000. The offspring of that marriage, Henry's father, grew up in that same little town and, at the age of seventeen, like his father, went back to Hong Kong to find a Chinese bride. That was in 1953. After his father found a bride and married, the couple also came back to Evanston, which is where Henry was born in 1955.

Recalling his grandfather's marriage, Henry said the wife he found must have come from a very wealthy family because his grandmother's feet had been bound and she couldn't walk. "She always had one or two whiskies at the end of the day, I remember, and her feet were very small and mangled. They must have been shortened by a couple of inches. She was from a class that had their women carried because they shouldn't have to walk," Henry explained. "She had two other sons besides my father—one who settled in Toronto and became very rich as the owner of the only tofu factory in the Chinese community there."

Though Henry's mother was in Hong Kong when his father found her, members of her family were already settled in the United States, including a sister in Los Angeles. In fact, after Henry's family visited that sister several times, his father eventually decided to move his family from Wyoming to California. He thought he could do much better if he opened his own Chinese restaurant in L.A.

Once settled in California, Henry had "a typical Chinese experience with aunts, uncles, and cousins close by—young cousins all playing together from dawn to dusk. When we were a little older we were always around the restaurant. We did our homework there after school and we helped out when my dad needed us for chores. I started working at the restaurant when I was eleven years old, and I worked there every Saturday until I went to college. My cousins and siblings did too. We were part of the extended community of L.A.'s Chinatown."

Henry's parents assumed he would focus on science and math, and he did not disappoint them when in high school he took courses that would prepare him for a pre-med concentration in college. Eventually becoming his high school's Pre-Med Club president, and volunteering every Sunday for three years to be a "candy striper" on the surgery ward of a local hospital, Henry thought he was on a straight path to becoming a doctor. Indeed after winning a full scholarship to the University of Southern California at Irvine, graduating with a B.S. in pre-med, he seemed on his way.

But then came another change. In his senior year, he "claimed his gay identity," he said, and moved to San Francisco. While making "lots of money waiting tables" there, he met someone who was moving to Boston. With that connection, Henry moved, too, getting a job as a trust officer in a Boston bank where he worked for the next nine years. Sometime in those years Henry met Robert Davis and the two married at 8:00 p.m. on the eighth day of the eighth month of 2008. "Eight is a lucky number for the Chinese," Henry said, "and we decided to celebrate in the tradition." Robert's last name became Davis-Wong.

Henry explained how his parents were about the marriage: "I didn't know much about my mother's family because she never talked about her past. Chinese people believe if there's a problem and you don't talk about it, it doesn't really exist. If you don't say something out loud, it isn't true. So that's how it was with my parents. It took my parents twenty-five years to invite Bob to lunch at their house in California."

How was it, I asked, that he who once planned to be a doctor now owned a dress shop in the South End? His mother was a seamstress, he said, and he had always been interested in clothes. "While at the bank I took a couple of night courses at Boston's School of Fashion Design in 1986, where I met two women who wanted me to join them to form a company. The three of us began our firm in a second-floor space on

Clarendon Street, selling wholesale clothing to Bonwit Teller, Bloomingdale's and other high-end retailers. We called the firm OKW after our three initials: one Chinese, one Jewish, and the third part Italian, part black, part Cherokee." Since 2009 the company has been on Tremont Street in the South End.

Henry said he gets up at 5:30 a.m. every day, is at the shop by 8:00 a.m., and works late. "I'm very Chinese. I work, work, work." He and Robert bought their house on Shawmut Avenue in 1982 and have been part of a closely knit group that has shared dinners and social occasions ever since. Recently the neighbors all had a cocktail party where they set up a kiddy pool in backyard and shared drinks and conversation around the deck. Last Halloween almost all the neighbors got dressed up and gave out about fifty pounds of candy to more than three hundred children.

The next time I met with Henry he said he had some surprising news. He and Bob were moving to California. It was time for a "new chapter" in his life, he said. He wanted to be near his family, and he would be glad to leave the New England winters. "Besides, we were part of the AIDS generation when so many of our friends died. It had a big impact on us. We want to spend more time together." I called Henry at OKW about three months after that conversation and the manager said he had already moved. "They've gone to Palm Springs," he told me, "but Henry has the same cell number."

So I called Palm Springs. They were already settled into a rented house and were looking to buy, Henry said. Everything was a lot cheaper than in Boston, but you have to drive every-where, even to pick up a pound of coffee or a dozen eggs. The city is sixty-two percent gay, he reported, and he and Bob will have a lot more living space than they could have in Boston. Those were the good points, but wouldn't they miss being on Haven Street with their old friends, I asked? "Our neighbors were fabulous. We love them, but now we are doing something else," he said. Just another change for someone not unaccustomed to making them!

— • —

Speaking of change: the South End has undergone countless changes, big and small, over its short 150-year history— a recent one being the appearance of dogs. When I moved onto Holyoke Street in 1978, there was one dog on my street. Today there may be as many as fifteen on that one block—not including the dog park at the end of the street which attracts dozens daily, hundreds in a month. The area was a basketball court for teens decades ago, just one clear indication of how the pet population has become a priority.

Jim Batty, another South End entrepreneur, has caught the tailwind of this change and has made a business out of it.

Jim Batty

The most popular items in K 9 on Pembroke Street are beef bones, pig's ears, and lamb bones—all eminently chewable. The customers making these items hot are owners of an impressive range of canine pets: bulldogs, boxers, retrievers, dachshunds, shepherds, corgis, and more. The cheery little dog that greets you at the door is part shih tzu, and part poodle. His owners—and owners of the shop—are Jim Batty and Daniel Avila.

I met with Jim one of those *cruel* April days when rainy cold can drain any zest you've managed to have the day before when it was a little nicer. Not Jim Batty's however. He'd made it through another month with the business growing, and he was in a good mood. While we spoke, Daniel was downstairs sitting with the handful of dogs that had come for a play date. Besides selling pet supplies (dogs only, for the moment) on the street floor, K 9 offers pet care services: solo walks, two- or three-hour play groups, day care, and grooming. Jim said they have as many as fifty different dogs over the course of a week in one or another of these activities.

When I met Jim in his shop, he talked about his business as a sign of the growth in the number of South End pet owners, but he was also eager to talk about the growth and change in the gay community as well. Gay men began moving into Boston in the early 1960s, and by the 1990s the city had a solid reputation as a community with a large gay population, he said. "Boston's Gay Pride Parade began in 1974 and continues to this day. I grew up in Wilmington, Delaware, and later went to the University of New Hampshire in Durham. I went through at least four majors, even thinking I might be a lawyer, but nothing seemed to stick. I was adrift." Then a friend at UNH told him he should "come out" and move to Boston because it was a good place for gays to live. After graduation in 1992 Jim did just that.

Once settled, he went into retailing, working at The Gap and then as manager at the Banana Republic on Newbury Street. For a short period he moved to California "to do the surfing thing and try life there," but he didn't like it enough to stay. While he was there, however, he met Daniel, who moved to the South End to live with him. The two, Red Sox fans, were married in November 2012 with fifty people attending the ceremony in Section 32 of Fenway Park.

Jim kept working at Banana Republic until 2012 when the couple decided to go into the business. They could do so because Daniel had developed a clientele as a full-time dog walker, and people seemed ready for more services. "We've only been in this shop since last fall, so it's pretty new," Jim told me. "It was a big step for me. I was afraid to quit my job because Daniel and I depended on it as steady income. But we both loved dogs and wanted to try opening a shop. So far it's been a successful venture." They've done a lot of juggling, and its always nip and tuck at the end of the month, but the business is growing and they love having it.

When I asked him what had he observed about the South End since he moved here in 1994, Jim said he thought a lot had changed for the gay community. When he arrived he felt he was coming to a community where a gay identity was an obvious and even welcome thing in the neighborhood. Now he wasn't so sure. "For example, there's a gay parade next week and you see some flags in shops, but twenty years ago, everybody was hanging flags in their windows. There were even banners on the streetlights advertising the parade. Now you don't see that so much. The shop owners, I think, hang the flags to try to keep a connection to the gay community mostly because they don't feel it's as strong as it used to be."

I asked why the change when the population in general was so much more accepting of gay people. "It might be because rents and property values are so high that only people with big incomes can afford to live here. There are a lot of young professionals here now, and several retired people from the suburbs who want to try city life, but these are not people that are strongly attached to the neighborhood. You can see it in small businesses on Tremont. A lot of them are struggling, and it's hard to hold on to a retail enterprise when people aren't really shopping here. A lot of gay people have moved out, either because the rents got too high or because they could now live openly in towns further out. Attitudes toward gays have changed and gays are accepted almost everywhere."

I commented that I had always found it interesting that Americans are such ardent dog lovers, while there are virtually no dogs in Eastern Europe, Africa and the Middle East. In China and India, where people do have dogs, they do not relate to them as we do. What is it that we love about dogs, I asked. Jim thought it had a lot to do with people just liking to take care of animals—buying them food, giving them exercise, taking them to the vet. Of course, they are companions, Daniel said, which made Jim add with a smile, "Another thing. You can get them to do what you want. You can tell them what to do and they do it. You can scold them and a couple of minutes later they want to crawl up on your lap. You can't do that with humans!"

Before I left the shop Jim took me down to see the dog play group. It was getting toward the end of the day and Daniel said at this hour he likes to let the dogs do what they're used to doing at home this hour. Sure enough, there they were, four different dog types, three big, one very little, all sprawled out on the couch watching TV. Great way, they seemed to say, to end the afternoon.

— • —

Speaking of dogs, Gayané Ebling was eager to tell me how her dog was helping her meet people in her neighborhood on Tremont Street around Boston Center for the Arts. It's a quickly changing area with new apartment buildings, an upscale wine shop, and clothing stores. She goes to nearby parks with her dog to meet people. It's easier to strike up a conversation with people you don't know if you both have dogs who are making friends, too, she said. She hadn't met Jim Batty yet, but my guess is it won't be long. She's only a few blocks down Tremont Street from his and David's shop.

Gayané Ebling

Gayané Ebling moved from a Victorian house in Newton to a floor-through condominium in the South End when her children were grown and she and her husband no longer wanted all the space of a big house. Besides, both wanted to live in the city. "Some people thought we moved to Baghdad," she said, laughing at their unfamiliarity with the city, "but we love it." A large percent of her friends in the South End are people she knew before the move, but she is slowly, slowly meeting new people. Her husband, who runs a software business, travels a lot of the time, so she is making inroads on her own.

Gayané grew up in an Armenian family of four children. Her mother is second generation Greek-Armenian from Lowell, Massachusetts, and her father is a first generation Armenian/Syrian who came to the U.S. to study at Massachusetts Institute of Technology. Although her parents raised the children in Lexington, they stayed deeply connected to their Armenian roots through a large extended family and their

Armenian church in Watertown. "I went to Sunday School but my education at church was mostly cultural, and I still have a familiarity with the language. Neither I nor my three siblings married an Armenian, but we were all married in the Armenian church, which tells you something!"

Although her parents accepted that their children would be Americanized, there were always reminders of her ethnic roots. "My grandmother wore black and we were taught certain values such as respect for older people and the importance of family dinners on Sunday. I used to dream of having a shag rug—probably turquoise—but we had only Oriental rugs all through the house. Our foods were mostly chicken, stuffed grape leaves, eggplant, and of course rice pilaf with every meal. My father was allergic to onion and garlic so my mother had to eliminate those Armenian staples, but she seasoned things with cumin, coriander, and other Middle Eastern spices.

Gayané skips over her professional life by saying that she worked in Washington, D.C., as a consultant for two years, then after a brief year in Boston, moved to New York for a marketing job at the Australian Trade Commission. Her family was very pleased, however, when she met her future husband, Tom, as their families were distantly related through marriage and, even more importantly, because Tom lived in Boston, which meant she would move back closer to her Armenian family.

While she was their raising their two children, Gayané did volunteer work, but in more recent years she had to put other things aside to take care of her aging parents. More and more people are needing to do that these days and it can be very consuming, she said, in her own case caring for her father, who was suffering from kidney disease, and for her mother, who was declining over a period of seven years with Alzheimer's disease. There's not only the task of understanding and following up on medical care, but being present almost the way you are with children.

She got certified to teach children with special needs and she has been volunteering in schools that need help, but now she also has more free time to travel, which has always been a passion. Mentioning just a few places she's been, including Italy, Morocco, Ethiopia, Kenya, Cambodia, and Vietnam, she ended with Armenia, where she and her husband took their children for a glimpse of their mother's heritage. "It was very beautiful, with hundreds of churches nestled into the countryside, but it was also very homogenous. People look alike and the old Armenian culture is pervasive. My father escaped to Syria to avoid genocide by the Turks and it is still very present in people's minds. In fact, the Cathedral of the Holy Cross in Boston recently held a service commemorating the Armenian genocide. I was among the eight hundred or more people that attended."

Gayané and her husband bought their third-floor South End condominium in an Art Deco building on Tremont Street near Berkeley before it was even built. Realizing it was a prime location where elegant Paris-style apartments were soon to materialize, they knew they couldn't go wrong. It was the new South End, and they were eager to try city living.

Many South Enders remember the one-story brick building that used to be in that spot: a nondescript structure that, over time, housed a White Castle restaurant, the Dover Tavern, a Gypsy reading room, Paul's Exports, and finally The Olde Dutch Candy and Antiques Store formerly located on Beacon Hill. In fact, it was the candy store owner and his partner, who, envisioning how lower Tremont and Washington Streets would soon change, undertook the development project, and created the Chevron Building where Gayané and her husband live. Curiously, the owner kept space on the street-floor space for a redone candy and antiques shop with much of the old dusty Beacon Hill ambiance. His goods include classic silver pieces, light fixtures, jewelry, paintings, and an extraordinary assortment of candy from lollipops to luxury chocolate bonbons.

Gayané said she loves living in the city and the diversity of people in the South End but she was very quick to add that in some ways living in the neighborhood has been difficult. Confessing that when she moved into the "new" South End, she couldn't avoid knowing that gentrification has meant that earlier residents have been displaced and forced to move away. It's nice to have all the convenience and pleasure of a pretty neighborhood, but the change will eventually undercut the way the South End has been. "I feel bad about it," she said.

— • —

Gayané's building borders the Berkeley Street Community Gardens where many of the South End's Chinese residents maintain fastidious plots packed with vegetables. I tried to interview someone from the large Castle Square housing development, where many of these gardeners live, but I couldn't get anyone to meet with me. Others had told me this might be the case so I went to meet the ebullient Franco Campanello at the Southwest Corridor Park bordering the Back Bay for a gardening story. Franco has a long and winding story that leads eventually to his stewardship of that park. Stretching from Back Bay Station to Massachusetts Avenue, the Southwest Corridor Park is punctuated with raised planters, tennis courts, tot lots, and community gardens. This public space offers activities and relaxation to hundreds of people each day. The gardens are Franco's domain.

Franco Campanello

Franco Campanello came to the Starbucks table where we planned to meet shaking his head. He had a cup of coffee in one hand and a plastic glass in the other. "They didn't just give me a glass of water," he said, "they had to write my name on a cup at the register and send it down to the serving area where they could deliver my own special glass with my name on it." He was frustrated. Once I knew more of his story, I saw why.

Franco grew up in a family of seven children. His father was a postal worker who worked two other jobs as well. "The nine of us lived in a small Hicksville, New York, Cape house with two bedrooms on the first floor. The rest of the house adapted as the family grew. "I was the middle child, lost among a bunch of loud siblings. You can know there were lots of boiled potatoes and constant food fights." He didn't escape until he went to college at the State University of New York, Stony Brook. His major then was marine biology. When I asked him why, he said probably because he wanted to "feed the world."

When Franco finished college he discovered he wasn't really interested in marine research so he taught junior high school in Commack, Long Island, for four years. "One of my students was the TV star Rosie O'Donnell," he said, "But that's another story. The main thing is, I didn't like teaching either so I moved to Boston. I was unhappy and struggling with coming out and I had to do something different. I knew Boston had a gay community at least. When I got here, I worked in a salad bar, then as a waiter and a cook."

When he eventually got a job at *C'est Si Bon* in Cambridge, the owner took Franco and the restaurant's chef to France and Italy for a tour he hoped would inspire his two top staff with new ideas. It worked. One of the restaurants they visited was a bistro in Bologna that had *torta rustica*. It set off a chain of memories, Franco said, that led him all the way back to home-cooked meals on Long Island. "My mom made *torta rustica* all the time," he said. "We called it 'garbage pie' because it was basically a crust with cheese and whatever else was around—ham, hard-boiled egg, broccoli—anything left over. Of course the cheese had to be ricotta, which is what made it so good."

When the three men got back to Boston, Franco said he started making *torta rustica* for the restaurant and pretty soon it was so popular they sold it as a side catering business as well.

Then one day, out of the blue, a friend suggested that Franco and his partner, Caleb Davis, open a restaurant. Which they did: the Calypso Cafe on Tremont Street in the South End.

"We didn't know what we were doing. Our lawyer told us we could raise money for a place by selling stocks, so we went up and down Tremont selling stocks to anybody who knew us and would buy. We were the *darlings* of the neighborhood at the moment, and we didn't worry. One couple offered $10,000 in bonds but when they asked us how and when we would repay, we had no answer. We had hand-drawn architectural plans so we went ahead and built the place ourselves. Someone told us we had to go to Inspectional Services but when we got there, people from the FBI were just sitting around with these guys, doing nothing, so we knew we didn't have to worry much about them. Those were the days in Boston when this kind of thing was common."

The restaurant was an instant success. Many people still remember it, but it was also a scary venture and may have been too much to take on too soon, Franco said. "The South End was still raw and kind of rough. A drunk would come in the restaurant and we'd have to haul him out or call the cops. Still, it was a time when you felt you could do anything. We did so much with so little in those days. For an inner-city neighborhood, we were unique. You could get an idea and go with it!"

After a couple of years, however, Franco said he got tired of making *torta rustica*. So he and Caleb and a third partner, Frank, decided to undertake a new venture—this time, a combination of cafe and health club. It was Franco's dream, he told me. He had visited San Francisco once and couldn't get over seeing gay bars where the people eating and drinking were visible from the street. Everything was closed off and gay life was supposed to be hidden in Boston.

So on the heels of the Calypso success, the three partners opened the Metropolitan Health Club and Club Café on Columbus Avenue. Although the two businesses eventually separated, Franco said his dream had come true. "Five years after I saw that bar in San Francisco, we had the first-ever place in Boston where gays could have drinks or lunch in front of windows open to the street."

Franco owned and operated the health club for twenty-three years but after a while it too got tiresome. He wanted something different. Without enough money to start another business, however, he took a real estate course in 2002 to become a broker. "It was awful work," he said. "People who do it are much underappreciated. I couldn't stay with it." In 2008 he began work as a concierge at the Marriot Copley Place where he has been ever since.

I met Franco when he moved to Holyoke Street in 1994. I would see him out in the postage-stamp front yard of his rental apartment trying to grow flowers with sparse sun and intrusive downspouts. We never got to talk long in those days, but years later, I started seeing Franco everywhere on the Southwest Corridor Park, now doing large-space gardening. I asked him one day how he got involved with the park.

"I have always needed a project, and when I saw how much the Corridor needed maintenance, I took it on. The park opened in 1990, but with water problems, dog abuse, and homeless people spending nights on the raised planters, it was showing serious wear by 1995."

As most long-term South Enders know, Southwest Corridor Park is the result of a hard-won victory when protesting Bostonians persuaded Governor Francis Sargent to cancel the construction of a new inner-city beltway and use the funds for public transportation projects. The 4.6-mile stretch that had already been cleared for the beltway became the new Orange Line and commuter Amtrak corridor with open space alongside or covering the tracks. That space became part of the Metropolitan Park System managed by the Massachusetts Department of Conservation and Recreation (DCR) and was quickly neglected. "The local DCR has been great, but the state has a massive park system, and the Corridor doesn't get enough resources. We kept pressuring them, but they kept cutting funds." It bothered him, he said, to see the Park so deteriorated.

True to his nature, he took the initiative. Bringing along other concerned neighbors, including Ann Hershfang, Betsy Johnson, and Lorraine Steele, he formed a group that became the non-profit Southwest Corridor Park Conservancy. Franco has been its president since 2007, and the work is all done by volunteers. "We prune the shrubs, take out the weeds and invasive plants, buy soil, prepare the beds, and do all the planting. There are about thirty-five people who help during different hours of the week." Franco works at least ten hours a week in the summer, in addition to fund-raising, which he does with a mailing to people on the neighboring streets. Last year the Conservancy brought in $10,000, all used for fencing, flowers, shrubs, trees, and truckloads of topsoil.

Among the trees is the gingko, whose fruit, Franco explained, has traditionally been eaten by the Chinese. "It's one of my favorite Park stories. All the trees put in by the city along the Corridor were male gingko trees. Then one day the trees started being female trees and bearing fruit. Since then, Chinese women have come over to the park to pick them. It's just one of the great things that happens on the Park."

Of course it's hard work maintaining a public space used by so many people. One project Franco has taken on recently is to make signs reminding pedestrians and dog walkers to be respectful of the landscaping. The sign at the end of my block says: "Plants grow by the inch and die by the foot. Please keep off the beds this spring." The wording has a definite Franco Campanello ring to it.

—•—

The Back Bay that begins on the other side of Franco's gardens looms large in Boston's history. Many have said that the appearance of the Back Bay, with grander and more elegant houses on Commonwealth Avenue and parallel streets, quickly upstaged its poorer cousin the South End. The two neighborhoods have often swapped populations, most recently in the 1980s when many Back Bay mansions were divided into small studios and apartments causing some residents to move to the South End for condominiums with more space.

But the Conines are going the other direction. When we first met, the couple told me they would be moving to the Back Bay in a year or so, did it matter for the book? Not at all, I told them. As a couple with young children, they belonged to a group of South Enders I was eager to hear from. Steve had made the Boston papers by selling a start-up that went public and sold at a dramatic profit. Neighbors told me Alexi had been a real force in making Titus Sparrow Park the lively, child-friendly park for countless individuals and families that is is today. They would give readers more perspective on their generation of South Enders.

Alexi And Steve Conine

I met Steve and Alexi Conine in their family dining room—the front of the parlor floor where you can see through the pantry to a large sunny kitchen beyond. It was the wall of the dining room, however, that immediately caught my eye. Covering a space about three-and-a-half feet wide and nine feet tall was what the Conines call a *Word Clock*—narrow strips of wood, each with a vertical alphabet that would slide up and down to settle into a horizontal copper frame displaying words sent from a hand-held computer. It's a Steve Conine invention, as is *Writer's Block*, a four-inch wood cube with a small lit screen on one side that flashes a new word every sixty seconds. His latest invention, Steve said, is several brass and silver-plate kinesthetic models demonstrating various mechanisms humans have invented over time to make moving parts: gears, cams, axels, etc. He made the pieces, each about a foot long and varying in heights, with an acetylene torch. There will be about twenty-four when he's done.

The patterned ceramic floor between the dining room and the kitchen is a mosaic by Alexi, an engineer by profession, artist by passion. The blown glass on the wood cabinet is her work, too, as well as goblets, landscapes of blown sea glass, and the leaded stained glass in panels of the front door. When she went to college, Alexi said, she had aptitude and an interest in both science and the arts, but finally settled on engineering as a practical option. Still, art is her main interest.

Alexi's neighbors know her for her work as president of Titus Sparrow Park—bringing about a cultural transformation in that green space by improving the lawn and playground, increasing the number of concerts from three to four a summer to fourteen, and instituting festive holiday celebrations: a pre-trick-or-treat party on Halloween, Santa and a piñata, an Easter egg hunt, and more. One event, a 2010 Victorian Jubilee celebrating the new cast-iron fence along West Newton Street, featured a ribbon-cutting ceremony that included music groups, carriage and pony rides, games, and a magician. About three hundred South Enders attended, many in Victorian dress, including top hats and parasols.

Steve and Alexi bought their Braddock Park house in 2001 with time to make changes in it before their three children were born in the years from 2004 to 2008. "When we bought it, the house was a two-family house so we changed it to be a one-family with my office on the top floor," Steve said. The office is where Steve and his partner, Niraj Shah, created Wayfair, a venture that would become the largest online retailer for home items and furniture in the country. It was the fourth start-up that Steve and Niraj began, and the one that made news in 2015 when the two partners sold a large percent of their shares for a reported $3–4 million.

I read about the company online and asked Steve how it had come about. His role, he said, was designing and implementing the programs that would set up the business for the internet. "I like solving problems and following them to the end. Give me a list or tell me 'get this built' and I can do it. I like doing things well, but I'm not a professional." I didn't know where one would draw the line.

I thought there had to be a background story to his acquiring this kind of know-how and when I asked Steve what it was, he answered with an anecdote. "I've always liked taking things apart to see how they worked. My baseball coach in grade school used to tell my family that when my brother would be out on first base scrambling after balls and trying to hit homers, I would be found in the stands, taking a ball apart to see how it was made."

Of course, family members had been powerful influences, too, not least his mother, who encouraged his urge to make from an early age, responding to any tool requests and even encouraging him to build his own workshop when he was in his woodworking phase around age twelve. His grandparents had a vegetable farm and he spent every summer there, helping and learning from his uncles—a couple of whom worked on old tractors to make them into hot rods for tractor-pulling competitions. "They let me into their workshops where I could see all their tools and watch them build their machines."

It contributed to his ongoing building obsession.

Alexi and Steve met at Cornell University where they were both studying engineering, Steve a year ahead of Alexi. She had lived in western Massachusetts (Stockbridge and Amherst) and felt like she grew up "in the country"—at least, in small towns. The last two years of high school she went to Miss Hall's School in Pittsfield where she got interested in horseback riding, but her greatest influence may have been her father, who though not a traditional breadwinner, she said, was whimsical and very devoted to her and was always interested in all her projects and proud of her achievements. That father loved words, Steve added, and was the inspiration for both the *Wall Clock* and *Writer's Block*.

When I asked how the two of them happened to settle in Boston's South End, Steve said he moved to the city in 1995 right after college to establish his first company with Niraj Shah. Later the two partners moved to London, where they took a couple of years to set up Wayfair. Eventually Alexi joined them and when she and Steve returned, they married and bought the South End house. "It seemed like nowhere at first," Steve said, but it was family friendly and they soon got active in the neighborhood.

The Braddock Park house has served them well, though rooms had changed purposes as they often do in the South End. The street floor, which had been a dining room in front and kitchen in back in the 1960s, was now a music room in the front with a guest bedroom in the back. The floor above the dining room and kitchen where the three of us met still had two bedrooms, but the top floor that was once was Steve's office is now a "costume" room in the back, and a bedroom in the front. Almost every room had some making going on: Legos, art projects, music. Steve has recently taken up the guitar—this, after he left off making 3D models. "They're easy," he said, "all you do is make the program and send it to a 3D printer and it's built!"

When Alexi first gave me their street address, I got a little shiver. I had been in that house countless times for Sunday brunches in the early 1960s when Father Bill Dwyer moved there from New York City to become vicar at St. Stephen's Church on Shawmut Avenue. I knew Bill and his wife Tako in New York and had moved to Boston at the same time, sending my things along in their van. I lived on Beacon Hill the next two years, from 1963 to 1965, but I got to know people in the South End and spent most of my time there so when I came back twelve years later, I made the neighborhood my home. That Braddock Park house held powerful memories for me.

— • —

Southwest Corridor Park, Titus Sparrow, Franklin Square and the many pocket parks of the South End all have their attractions, but there's one "secret" park few know about beyond the occupants of the houses that border it: Montgomery Park, a green-space gem without an alley or parking area to break up its trimmed lawn and graceful shade trees. Alphonse Litz lives on the park and enjoys it for its beauty, but also because it has helped him become acquainted with his neighbors. He has a project, however, that takes him far beyond the park into all corners of the South End. When we met it was almost all he wanted to talk about.

Alphonse Litz

The sound of hammers, saws, sanders, and young kids calling for supplies filled the room. It was the last day of Boston Explorers summer camp and most of those busy at work were finishing up a small pine table they had made from scratch over the preceding weeks. Some had already started to paint. In the midst of all the noise, a nine-year-old boy sent out the alert that the blue paint can was empty. He was working on a design for the surface of his table and desperately needed the depleted blue paint.

One of the adults stepped forward immediately and asked for the empty can. He'd go to the hardware store, he said, and get some right away. The adult was Alphonse Litz, founder and director of the 2013 Explorers camp that had been under way in Union United Methodist Church on Columbus Avenue for the previous four weeks. Alphonse's response to the supply emergency was typical of his single-minded commitment to the camp. Choosing not to interrupt counselors helping the kids, Alphonse was off on his bike for the paint.

When I visited, the camp was in its third year of operation. It began as a one-week pilot program for eleven kids in 2011 and had grown to be a four-week program with seventy-two children from across Boston: Dorchester, Mattapan, Jamaica Plain, as well as the South End. Alphonse describes the ideas that distinguish the camp in a brochure to parents:

> Every day, campers do four things: they make things with their hands, explore Boston (high and low, offshore and on, by bike, boat and T), have fun, and treat everyone with kindness. We want kids to learn to make choices for themselves and to do things for themselves that many of them have never had a chance to do in school.

Besides places nearby like the Christian Science reflecting pool and outdoor sculpture exhibits, the Prudential Tower look-out, and the Huntington Theater, campers visit Singing Beach, the Garden of Peace Memorial at the State House, Spectacle Island, the Old State House, and more. Older campers spend an overnight on Peddocks Island. Alphonse said the church is base camp, but Titus Sparrow is where everyone gathers to start the day, and where kids play games, have outdoor meals, and depart for their bicycle trips.

Alphonse grew up in Syracuse, New York, son of a Polish father and Italian mother. "The 1960s and 70s were a great time to be in a neighborhood like ours. All the houses were close together, many with two or three families, everyone related to each other one way or another. We played in the street and hung out in neighborhood centers, parks, and school lots. I went to a neighborhood Catholic school where five of my cousins were attending, too. A Polish great uncle, his wife, and their five children lived next door," he told me. His Polish grandfather played violin in the Syracuse Symphony Orchestra and his grandmother, who had not gone to school past the sixth grade, became a buyer for a local department store. Alphonse's Italian grandparents managed a mini-farm with a flourishing vegetable garden, fruit trees, and flocks of chickens, quail, and homing pigeons.

"I remember watching my grandmother tie a chicken to a tree and cut off its head," Alphonse recalled, musing on the simple actions borne out of age-old necessities. "My grandfathers used to compare gardens, and we always had great food!" That grandfather made Italian sausages; the Polish uncle made kielbasa. "My Polish grandfather made vodka and the Italian grandfather made grappa and wine. My dad told me that during the Depression everyone made bathtub gin."

Syracuse was an industrial city in those days and Alphonse remembered it as a vibrant community where corporate wealth was used for public benefit in the form of handsome buildings, parks, and a lively downtown shopping district. But in the 1980s, as industries moved their operations overseas, he said the city "lost its steam." Today the department stores that once thrived are closed, downtown has lost its vitality, and the population has dropped from 300,000 to just over 150,000.

Watching the city's demise made a powerful impression on him, especially as a 1970s adolescent planning for the future.

Maybe that impact was one factor that caused Alphonse and a friend to skip school for a couple of days during their junior year in high school and take a trip to Northampton, Massachusetts, where the friend's brother was in college. From there, Alphonse decided go on to Boston, hitching a ride on the college rugby team's bus for this last leg. "When I got to Boston, I saw Franklin Park and the Hancock and the Christian Science Church and I said I'm going to come back some day and stay."

After graduating from high school, Alphonse went on to the State University of New York (SUNY) at Genesco for three years, then transferred to Boston Architectural College in Boston, living in an apartment above Pizzano's Wood-working shop on Columbus Avenue. He loved the South End but didn't take to architecture, so he returned to SUNY for a teaching degree and then landed a job in a high school. After a time, however, he realized he preferred to work with younger children, so, saving money from house painting, carpentry, substitute teaching, and odd jobs, he returned to school to get a master's degree in elementary education. His first job in that field was teaching fifth grade in Concord, Massachusetts, where he stayed for seven years.

Meanwhile, he and a friend had bought an old house in Dorchester, restoring it by working on it evenings and week-ends. Alphonse liked living in the city but was growing weary of the daily commute to Concord. Eventually he looked for a school nearby and finally took a job close to home at the Mission Hill School. Mission Hill was a pilot program of the Boston Public Schools, in which teachers had a great deal of autonomy, allowing them to be creative in their teaching practices. It turned out to be the perfect place for Alphonse.

Given such latitude to develop their own calendar, courses, and budget, administrators and teachers crafted a curriculum that focused on the children's interests, cultivating those interests while exposing students to the world beyond their immediate communities. At a time when Boston Public Schools were sharply cutting their budgets and eliminating art, shop, and music classes, Mission Hill had them all. In fact, the school had gained such a reputation, Alphonse was reassigned to the Tobin School to expose faculty there to the Mission Hill model.

Unfortunately, it didn't work out that way. When Alphonse got to the Tobin, he was told his job was to help teachers improve their students' standardized tests scores. This was 2008, when many American educators believed testing would establish higher educational standards and help U.S. students better compete with achievement levels in other countries. Alphonse found that rather than helping teachers stimulate children's interests and natural curiosities, he was spending eighty percent of the school day talking about testing. One day, visiting a classroom, he heard a third-grader describe him as "the man who brings us the tests." Alphonse realized he was working against his principles and decided he would leave. The pleasures and satisfactions of working with children, however, did not leave him. Within a year of leaving the Tobin, Alphonse conceived of Boston Explorers.

Alphonse would have been happy to talk about Explorers more, but I was curious what he did in the off-season when he wasn't planning for the next season or fund-raising. To appease my curiosity, he suggested I visit the house on Montgomery Street that he and his partner, Bob Ditter, bought in 1996.

Montgomery Park, the only fully enclosed, commonly held open space in the South End is a beautiful half-acre garden with a lawn, trees, bordering flower gardens, and small groupings of tables and lawn chairs. It was not always so, however. Homeowners who bought in the 1960s can remember when it was a dump for old refrigerators, cars, washing machines, trashed cupboards, mattresses, not to speak of tossed medicine and liquor bottles, broken dishes, and old clothing. Even in the 1990s, Alphonse said, some of the wooden fences people had put up decades before were still there, as well as telephone and cable lines that had not yet been sunk underground. Today it's one of the most coveted green spaces in the South End, maybe the city. Homeowners on all four bordering streets know how lucky they are to have their backyards blend into this jewel of a park.

Alphonse is the park's outdoor electrical and mechanical maintenance man, keeping gas lamps, fountains and locks operating properly, but his other occupation outside Boston Explorers has been to transform his and Bob's house on Montgomery Street. A badly neglected, decaying brick house with bare-bones electrical wiring and antiquated plumbing when they bought it, Alphonse has been slowly transforming it from a dingy, cramped, jerry-rigged rooming house into a handsome four-story townhouse with a rental bed and breakfast unit and workshop on the garden level, a client waiting room and office for Bob's consulting practice on the street floor, and sunny living areas above. When I visited, there were boards on the second-floor landing where Alphonse was still making moldings and woodwork for places where the originals had rotted beyond hope of restoration. In the dining room he had removed bricks to lower the frames of windows facing the park. It had taken countless hours of scraping walls, stripping woodwork, sanding, plastering, tiling, and painting, but he enjoyed the work and the place was "getting there."

When we finished going through the house, Alphonse wanted to return to the subject of the park that has been such an important feature in his sense of community and social life. "The park's bordered by thirty-six other buildings, about eighty-six households in all. It's great for kids and adults alike but at the same time," he said, he has noticed a change. Many people living on the park now don't spend the year there, and almost everyone is gone in the summer. Some people use their houses as a second or third home and don't feel connected to the park or neighborhood at all. "They hire florists or nurseries to do their window boxes and yards. We're in another time of transition. Class has made an impact. We feel it a lot," he said, wistfully.

— • —

Alphonse has a sense of belonging to the whole area when he speaks of the South End because Boston Explorers is based there and many South Enders support the program, but most residents are more inclined to refer to a very limited group of streets as their "neighborhood." Some of those groupings have names such as Cosmopolitan, Ellis, Blackstone/Franklin, Pilot Block—at least a dozen in all. Of all the clustered communities, however, Villa Victoria may be the one with the most significant history.

In the 1960s, when Boston's Urban Renewal plan was calling for a massive rebuilding of the city, the South End was targeted for large swathes of aging houses to be demolished and replaced with new construction. One of the swathes was Parcel 19, the area between Shawmut Avenue and Tremont Street from Worcester Street to West Dedham Street—an area occupied almost entirely by newly arrived Puerto Ricans and some Cubans. The fight to save their place in the neighborhood became legendary, with countless demonstrations and protests over several years. The people of Parcel 19 prevailed. Residents of the area formed the non-profit Inquilinos

Boricuas en Acción (IBA) that eventually developed 895 low-to moderate-income units for 3,000 residents—almost all of whom previously lived in the neighborhood.

I met Carmen Morales and her daughter Elsa Morales in the tot lot and pocket park called Cityscape III on Newland Street. The two were watching Niko, Elsa's grandson. Carmen and Elsa both have apartments in adjacent buildings on a street one block away from the Villa proper, but both said they belong to the Villa community. Carmen said she attended the meetings and was part of the struggle to get it built.

Carmen And Elsa Morales

Carmen Morales was born in Puerto Rico but moved to the U.S. with her two little boys in 1964 to find work. At first she lived with an aunt but eventually moved out when the uncle, with his "macho ways," made it difficult. Carmen came from a family of seven children, eventually having six children of her own—four girls and two boys.

"The South End was a disaster when I first came. It looked like a tornado had hit it, very run down," Carmen recalled. Her aunt's apartment was on Upton Street in an area occupied by mostly Italians, Syrians, and Lebanese, but she soon connected with fellow Puerto Ricans living in Parcel 19. In fact, even while raising young children, working in a factory and at late-night security jobs, she joined Bill Bradley, Father Bill Dwyer, and others who organized to ensure residents in Parcel 19 were not permanently displaced. "We had to fight. We had to picket and go to endless meetings, but we finally got it done," Carmen said. She moved into her own place on West Concord Street in 1972. It is part of the package that IBA settled with the city.

"It was hard when I first came here," Carmen told me. "I didn't know the language. I had to ask questions about everything and figure out what people meant. Finally I got to take a class in English for a year." Though she was busy with the children those early years, when the younger ones were old enough to go to the Mackey School, she finally got a job she really liked as a teacher's aide. Then in 1979 she had to change her life again. Her older son was grown and had two children of his own, but the mother had problems that meant she could no longer keep the children. Carmen's son said he would support the family, but asked if she could take them in to live with her. "I couldn't let the children go to some foster home. That would be terrible. I took them and raised them too. God was my help."

Carmen's daughter Elsa was born in 1967 and remembers living on Tremont Street before the family moved to West Concord Street when she was five. Her memories of growing up were of going to the Hurley School and then to Boston High, located in Copley Square at the time, with everyday life totally focused on the Villa—"hanging out with friends in the neighborhood. There used to be a basement room at 630 Tremont and teenagers would all go there to party and dance on Friday and Saturday nights. I was always with my friends in the Villa. We were all together then."

Elsa started working when she was in high school, getting

her first job in a summer program at IBA when she was fifteen. Later she worked in the mail room at a bank, in a coffee shop, and then at Filene's Basement. Then, at age twenty-one, she began her own family and got her own place. Over the years she has lived in three different apartments, but always in Rutland Housing on Worcester Street where her mother lives. "With subsidized housing, the number of bedrooms is determined by the number of children. I had a boy and a girl but when they got older and moved out, I had to move back to a one-bedroom," she said.

I asked both Carmen and Elsa how they felt about the neighborhood these days. Carmen said her friends all lived in the Villa and she still thought of that as her community. Even now she goes over to play bingo and visit friends there. With her calm and friendly manner I guessed she was well-liked by just about everyone. She said yes, she has been lucky. "I feel fifteen years old and my friends often tease me that I look like I am." It's true. She pulls her dark hair back, Spanish flamenco-dancer style, and wears long trimmed fingernails painted in a youthful turquoise. Still, it was easy to see that experience had made her quiet and reflective. "I know everybody, I've been here so many years. Some people you like and some you don't but it's your community and eventually you accept everyone."

Elsa's experience has been different. Things have changed for her and most people her age have moved away. She said she keeps to herself. "The neighborhood looks better, it's cleaner, there's lots of parks where the elderly can sit and be with people they know. There's community rooms for the elderly too and things they can do. That's good." But Elsa said it just isn't the same. The Villa has far fewer Puerto Ricans now, with more Chinese and Southeast Asians instead. "They don't mix with other people much. But it's also that people don't let their kids out to run around on their own like they used to. Parents keep them in their apartments." People used to look out for one another and now it seems they don't so much. She also wondered about the younger generation. "It feels like they don't want to work that hard to get what they want. They're into styles and having things but when we grew up we all knew you had to get jobs and work hard to get what you wanted. They don't seem to want to do that."

I told Elsa I thought there was less violence in the West Newton Street area than there had been a decade or two ago. She said things went in cycles and that the neighborhood would be quiet for a while and then a new cycle of violence would erupt, "just like clothing styles and all the rest." She was frustrated about the way parenting had changed and about how parents can't enforce rules on their children or discipline them the way they did in the past. Maybe it is society and maybe it is the government, she didn't know. But it seems there are restrictions everywhere you turn. Sometimes a person "has the heart to take in a child but there's all kinds of rules—on single people, on gays, on lots of people. It is difficult," Elsa said. She works these days as a personal care assistant, and likes to help people, but she stays private. "I don't socialize and go visit. The only person I visit is my mom."

I had met Elsa and Carmen through a neighbor who told me her son had been on a baseball team that Elsa coached. When I asked Elsa about it, she smiled and said yes, she started a baseball team when her son was young and recruited others to join. In fact, she coached young kids in the Villa for fifteen years and clearly loved it. She became the first female umpire for the South End teams and was recommended for the Jamaica Plain league, too. Those were the good days.

Elsa and Carmen both speak Spanish and English fluently, but they had showed a certain reticence when we first met. At the end of our first conversation they told me why. Tragedy had recently struck the family. Elsa's son Niko Esai was shot and killed in the South End on July 14, 2014. The assailant was unidentified, though Elsa says someone may know and not want to talk. Carmen said, "Niko was only twenty years old and used to come into my house a lot to see me or get something to eat. I pray every day that I won't die until they find the person who did it." Elsa, who had only Niko and a daughter, said she can't talk about it. It's all been too devastating.

— • —

I hardly knew Arnold Zack when we met in his West Canton Street living room one April morning in 2014, but I had noticed him at the South End Seniors, an ad hoc group that meets to discuss local and sometimes national news every Tuesday. Arnold had a particular way of offering his opinion or refuting others that struck me as measured and unimpassioned. His positions were always well backed up with facts but he seemed uninterested in winning an argument. It was so noticeable that I wanted to how and where he had acquired this skill. I soon learned.

Arnold Zack

Arnold Zack has spent more than fifty-five years arbitrating and mediating with more than five thousand national and international contenders. He has been in the middle of disagreements between countless institutions, including municipal governments, teacher unions, police departments, postal services, transit systems, and scores of private companies trying to reach wage or contract agreements. Four U.S. presidents have called on him for his expertise: Jimmy Carter, George H. W. Bush, Bill Clinton, and Barack Obama. His career spans from the 1950s, when the court systems were the exclusive means of settling disputes, to the present, when mediation and arbitration are globally recognized as one of the most economical and effective ways to solve conflict. It's a personal and professional success story.

I began our conversation by asking Arnold about his immediate engagements. He would soon be off to an International Labor Organization meeting in Geneva, where judges and tribunal representatives from at least twenty or more international organizations would discuss due process guarantees. Also upcoming were trips to China and Bangladesh, where he has been consulting. He would have meetings with various branch members of the International Monetary Fund, the United Nations, and the World Bank as well. And last but not least, he would be teaching in the Labor and Work Life program at Harvard Law School, as he has done for thirty years.

A few years ago, Arnold wrote an autobiography, *Arnold Zack from A to Z.* He wrote it, he explained, mostly because his wife Norma had wanted their children to have a record of his travels and projects. He didn't do it until after his mother's death, when he found old letters full of names and dates and details of his earlier decades. I said that I had read the book but he quickly interrupted to say, "Oh, I wrote that back in 2007 when I was in my 70s. Things were just getting started then. The years since then have been the exciting ones."

He gave the following as an example of his new work: "Before the 1948 [Chinese Communist] Revolution, all the goods we were making got shipped to China. Now everything is made there and shipped back to us: shoes, clothes, refrigerators, computers. It's a huge shift in global manufacturing, but in China they have nobody representing the workers' side in disputes. Workers have resorted to "boss nabbing" as a way to make their demands heard, but through a joint effort with Massachusetts Institute of Technology and business-related schools in China, a team of us are setting up mediation training for future managers to use before disputes escalate to strikes or economic and political trouble."

Arnold had done similar work in South Africa, beginning back in 1985 when the apartheid regime was still in power. Making more than forty trips over the next fifteen years, he helped leaders identify unions that the new government could work with, and develop mediation and arbitration programs for labor-government disputes. Finally, he helped ensure that the new post-apartheid government institute a Commission for Conciliation, Mediation, and Arbitration. "It is now the only government in the world providing all employees with mediation and arbitration services for termination disputes."

How did he happen to get into the arbitration field and then extend it to the work he was doing now, I wondered. This is where his autobiography came in handy. It told Arnold's family history and early life.

His paternal grandfather, he writes, worked as a peddler when he first came to America, and Arnold's father, Samuel Zack, was the first in their Jewish family to be educated. After finishing two years of university to do so, Sam Zack attended Suffolk Law School, all the while working nights in a Lynn shoe factory and commuting to Boston for day classes.

Sam graduated but did not practice law for long. He had been active in local politics, and through a colleague in Washington, D.C., he was asked to help draft legislation that gave workers the right to unionize. This legislation created the 1935 National Labor Relations Board (NLRB) to settle disputes. Eventually Sam was called to work for the Board as a regional chief attorney, so he moved the family to the Philadelphia area.

Sadly, Sam Zack had a near-fatal heart attack only four years after the move, making it necessary for the family to move back to Massachusetts—this time to Brookline where Arnold's brother, Michael, was born shortly after. With his father ill, the family's financial future was uncertain. Arnold entered the Brookline schools but, even in middle school, was babysitting, washing windows, and selling newspapers to help meet the family expenses. Once at Brookline High, he got a regular job selling shoes, which perhaps partly explains why he wrote in his autobiography that his high school years were "hazy" and he didn't get involved in many activities.

That would change when he got to Tufts University. Although his father died in his first year and he had more responsibilities at home, he got active in a number of organizations, including the 1952 Adali Stevenson campaign for president. In his senior year he applied and was accepted at Yale Law School, a choice he said he would never regret. Though the social milieu was something he had never known before, and he had to work at jobs while many students didn't, Yale was an invaluable experience. "I was studying at one of the best law schools in the country and I made life-long friends." Most importantly, he gained the attention of Saul Wallen, president of the Nation Academy of Arbitrators (NAA). It was Wallen who gave Arnold his first post-graduation job at the Academy headquarters in New York, and it was Wallen who suggested he apply to the Littauer Center, now the Kennedy School of Government at Harvard, to broaden his contacts for international work. Arnold told me he knew by then that he wanted a career in labor relations—and he wanted to see the world!

It is no wonder then, that as a Littauer student Arnold wanted to attend a Communist Youth Festival in Vienna. In retrospect, it's hard to cipher just what he knew and when, but it was at the Festival that he met Russian exiles and Africans who eventually got him connected to Radio Free Europe, a CIA affiliate that was part of the U.S.'s secret network spying on the Soviet Union in African countries. The Cold War dominated American policy during this period, and the government told Radio Free Europe it was interested in "anything Zack could do to fill in the information gap on Africa." The CIA involvement was short-lived, however, and when President Kennedy announced he would establish the Peace Corps in 1960, organizers asked Arnold to help recruit blue-collar workers and students on college campuses. When he later returned to Africa, he did so to set up trade-union training schools. In1967, he returned to work permanently at the NAA again, traveling between New York and Boston for work with clients Saul Wallen contracted for him.

Around this time, Arnold met Norma Wilner, a Barnard graduate who had finished medical school at the University of Pennsylvania and was beginning a fellowship at the New England Medical Center in Boston. As both Arnold and Norma tell the story, the idea of a romance between them occurred to their mothers first, when the two older women discussed their children at a relative's wedding but it was Norma who, on the Vineyard one weekend after they had been dating a few months, asked with her typically wry sense of humor, "Have we decided to get married?"

The place on the Vineyard where Norma proposed was in Gay Head on a property where Arnold had built a house with friends back in 1964. "It was a time when you could do things like that on the Vineyard," he said. He and Norma had their first honeymoon there and still spend summers with family on the island. The second honeymoon was a trip to Africa.

Arnold and Norma had been married for a year when they started thinking about places to live that would be good for raising a family. Arnold suggested the South End, where he and some friends had bought an old Appleton Street rooming house in 1962 as a "cheap place to live." The group found they had doubled their initial investment when they sold the house five years later so Arnold lobbied with Norma for the South End. She wanted to settle in Brookline where their children could go to better schools. They came to a tentative agreement when Norma said she'd try the South End for a year. That was more than four decades ago. The children have grown up and live in other cities, but Arnold and Norma are still in the same South End bowfront. They said they love the house for the history they've had in it as a family, and for the many neighbors who have become friends. They do not plan to move soon!

Aileen Thomson frequents the Tremont Street Starbucks and the first time I noticed her was a drizzly February day when she was wearing a long, faded blue denim skirt with a largish plaid shirt and reading a newspaper. A week or two later I saw her there again, this time outside locking her bicycle to a parking meter. The bike was decorated with plastic flowers around the basket, a sign, I thought, of someone with a quirky sense of humor. I had seen the bike a few times near the weekend flea market at the corner of Tremont and Rutland Square, so that second Starbucks morning I introduced myself and asked if she lived in the South End. If so, would she be willing to talk to me about the neighborhood and her life. Her answer was a ready yes to both.

Aileen Thomson

When I had my first conversation with Aileen Thomson, I noticed she had an accent. She pronounced certain one-syllable words: *hay-ad* for *had, ay-und* for *and* and, *ee-its* for it's. I began by asking her the origins of her accent. She was born in north-central Scotland, she said, her father was a farmer, her mother an employee in a law office. Their land was very flat and good for growing grains, but not thickly settled yet, though Edinburgh was not far away. "Glaciers had leveled the land except for certain high places, which is where castles were built later," she said. She was an only child and "left to grow up like I wanted." After finishing "the grades," she went to St. Andrews University, later transferring to Dundee University for a degree. She thought she would be a teacher, but jobs were scarce. "The only jobs I could get were taking care of children. My sights were higher!"

It was no surprise that she decided to come to the United States, initially using what experience she had to work as a nanny. Her first job was with a wealthy Milton family who had famous houseguests like Averill Harriman. "It was endlessly fascinating," Aileen said. The husband, from an old Yankee family, had been lost over the Pacific during the war. His wife, a former Olympic skier, was an avid vegetarian, growing her own food and having the rest sent from places where it was certified as "pure." Once the wife ordered a box of praying mantises to eat insects in her garden so she wouldn't have to use insecticides. "Everything was expensive and there was no concept of saving, which was all new to me. I enjoyed it and stayed a few years."

Eventually, however, she took a job at the Bank of Boston, moving to Appleton Street in the South End and enrolling at University of Massachusetts, Boston, in political science. The neighborhood was very "dicey" for a young single woman in the late 1960s, Aileen said, but she loved its excitement. "I was very social and up for everything. Two clubs I remember were Conley's and the Pioneer—both places for jazz. You had to know somebody to go to the Pioneer. It was on the other side of Massachusetts Avenue on the third floor of an old building, but very chic."

After the bank job, Aileen worked for a urologist at Brigham Hospital. He was "a character, ambitious and frequently in arguments with board members and colleagues." At one point he bought a hotel in Maine, Aileen said, where he wanted to set up a Scotch 'N Sirloin restaurant; at another point, he split with his wife, remarried, and then opened some sex therapy clinics. When companies like Eli Lilly began massive clinical trials, the doctor got involved with testing catheters. "It was balderdash really, just about getting enough people for test numbers. When a doctor in Pittsburgh began doing liver transplants, my employer moved there and I went, too. I was in the middle of everything, taking on tasks from ordering wine for the restaurant to keeping records on the clinical trials."

Eventually she decided to leave and move back to the South End, where she had always loved living. But soon after returning she was diagnosed with uterine cancer. "It was a disease that most people thought, in those days, could never be cured. People I knew had strange responses to my news," she said. "Some were kind, some very generous, but others were nosy. People seemed to come out of the woodwork and suddenly want to help but mostly people had very old-fashioned ideas about the disease. A couple suggested I go back to Scotland to die."

It wasn't in Aileen's nature to give up, however, and after treatment, she was soon free of the disease, though it would take some time to get over it emotionally. "People told me sometimes it doesn't hit you until months later, and that was what happened to me." At one point she did return to Scotland, thinking she might want to settle there, but the U.S. and the entrepreneurial spirit had taken root and she came back, enrolling in Northeastern University for a master's degree in business administration. Posting her qualifications on monster.com, Aileen told me the calls for interviews came flooding in. She was soon back to work and bought a condo on the

South End's Hanson Street.

Aileen's real passion, she told me, is the buying and selling of things. "It's in my blood, I guess. In Scotland we had "rag and bone men" who used to collect discards and peddle them on the streets and roads and I remember them." It's not exactly what she is doing herself, but for years now, she has been buying at flea markets, yard sales, and second-hand stores and then reselling her purchases. One of her favorite places to buy is the Goodwill Outlet, which is in the building behind the regular Goodwill on Washington Street in Roxbury. Aileen told me she can spend less than $5 on things that she knows right away someone else would be happy to buy for more. "There are all kinds of people at Goodwill—dealers, poor people, rich people, doctors from the hospital. I just spend an hour or so, but I always pick up something." If she's successful, it's because she has an eye for what people might want. "It's like a sixth sense," she said.

Aileen's entrée into selling came when a friend who owned a house on Hanson Street wanted to have a garage sale for things tenants had left behind. "She asked me to help, so one Saturday morning we put all the items out on the sidewalk. I watched my friend sell tables with missing legs, broken chairs, an old iron—all kinds of stuff. She made out like a bandit! It was an eye-opener for me, another American thing I didn't know." The two women went out for dinner to celebrate. A few weeks later, Aileen and a couple of others set up another sale on Hanson Street that did just as well. Soon they were in business.

Aileen told me that eventually she started selling rare books on eBay, which is where she does most of her selling now—everything from high-end, contemporary clothing and expensive handbags to trinkets and costume jewelry. Not long ago she sold a rare Dutch tile to Eton College Library in England, which holds a collection that needed her piece to be complete. "People pay me through PayPal and I have it set up so the money goes directly into my brokerage account." I commented that I guessed she had put away quite a bit by now. Grinning, she told me it's a lot harder for her to spend money than save it.

The last time we had a conversation, someone had stolen her bike. She had to get a new one, at Goodwill of course. "But the lock costs way more than the bike, almost $100. It's me, a non-professional bike rider against professional bike thieves, and they win." While we spoke, several people coming into Starbucks greeted her. At one point she waved to a woman walking into Casa Cuong across the street on West Canton. I commented that she seemed to know a lot of people in the neighborhood. "Hmm, well, yes, I guess I do," she said with the same bemused smile she had when she told me about professional bike thieves.

— • —

Most of the people profiled in this collection were able to talk about several years of life experiences. Indeed, some could speak of many decades. Sean Curry falls into a generation gap that comes between parents of the 1960s and 1970s, whose children have grown up and left the neighborhood, and young parents whose children have been born in the new millennium. During the South End's 1980s and 1990s, much of its housing was being converted to apartments and condominiums with new tenants who were either single or couples. I was pleased when Sean agreed to speak with me as I had been hard-pressed to find young people of his generation.

Some say a child's basic character and personality are shaped by the age of seven. I was way too late meeting him to know if that saying was true in his case, but Sean didn't change much over the times we met. He had a striking number of contrasting experiences during that time, but he seemed very much himself throughout—polite, clear-headed, and somewhat reserved. Here's his story so far.

Sean Curry

Sean Curry has lived on the South End's West Canton Street all his life. His mother is was born in the Philippines but later moved with her family to Hawaii, which is where she met her husband when he was stationed at the Air Force base there. When I first met Sean, he had just finished his freshman year at Bentley University in Waltham. He didn't have a lot to say about his school and life, however, and I felt like he hadn't quite settled in to being a college student. He was reticent.

He did, however, get more animated once he began talking about kung fu, the discipline he has practiced for the past ten years. "I could only come into Boston two or three times a week for practice when I was in school this year, but now that it's summer I go four or five times a week," he told me. Though he has had lots of different teachers, there is one *shifu* who is always at the class and who gets to know the students and talks to them about their lives. "It's a lot less formal than you think," Sean said, assuring me that even though the discipline is rigorous, the atmosphere is casual. When I asked what he thought was the greatest benefit he said without hesitation, "It keeps my mind clear. It's all about being focused. When I go to a session with a lot on my mind, by the time I come out, my head is absolutely clear."

Sean went to the Josiah Quincy School for grade school and Boston Latin for grades seven to twelve. Taking mostly science and math courses, he knew by the time he got to college that he wanted to study finance and business. I asked him if he thought he wanted a field with a secure future and he said, "Maybe that, too." He seemed to have something else in mind though he didn't say so.

In that first interview Sean told me he "wasn't doing much" that summer. "I watch TV a lot but I don't do Facebook or text. I work two times a week, usually from 6:00–9:30 p.m. at Coda Restaurant on Columbus, but I'm not doing sports or anything. I played football in high school and I liked it but I don't do it now." I asked him if he reads and he said, "No, not really. If I read a book it'd be about business and finance but it's hard to find those books just to read." At the end of our somewhat "paused" conversation he said that he guessed he liked "things to be routine."

When I met Sean ten months later, he had a Mohawk haircut and a thick black beard that extended at least an inch below his chin. He also seemed more eager to talk. For one thing, he had just returned from a two-and-a-half week job where he and forty-seven other Bentley students conducted orientation sessions for new students who would be starting in the fall. Twice as many had competed for the job, so the "winners" felt lucky and quickly bonded, especially as they spent a week together in training. "We got to know each other really well. It was like being on a retreat where you did team-building exercises to find out things about each person." After it was over, someone made a phone app so they could all stay in touch. It gets as many as 1,000 hits a day, mostly inside jokes that only the group could get. Sean still doesn't do Facebook or Twitter but he does read notes from those friends.

I asked Sean if the second year at Bentley was different from the first. He was still doing kung fu but only once a week this year, he said. Last year he went to a tournament in Baltimore where participants competed on particular "forms." The name of his discipline was Wah Hunu Tam Tui Praying Mantis and he had done well. At school this year, he got to choose his housing. His suite, shared with six friends, had a common room where they could all hang out. "I was more social," he said, "but studied more, too."

"I took two courses on American government, politics, macroeconomics, and current events, and also started taking more courses in my major. I loved my accounting course. We wrote summary analyses of case studies and learned how to make financial analyses for investments. You can get by without reading the text, but I read them all for all my classes. I took the CLEP (College Level Examination Program) exams, too." In fact, he got As or A minuses in all of his classes, though I had to ask to learn that.

Sean didn't have much to say about growing up in the

South End. He went to St. Cecelia's Sunday School when he was young and joined kids there for trips to Florida and Montana, where he worked with Neighbors in Action, but the St. Cecilia's kids were from South Boston and Charlestown and they had their own friends from the neighborhood. "In Charlestown, it was like every kid knew every other kid his own age. There weren't that many kids in the South End and we didn't all hang out together like they did other places."

Sean's big news was that he would be studying in Hong Kong for the coming fall semester in an exchange program that Bentley has with Hong Kong University. He had been to Hawaii several times to visit his mother's family, but otherwise hadn't traveled. After three weeks of working with his father in Hawaii, he said, he would go straight to Hong Kong.

When he got back from Hong Kong he told me the university had kids from all over so it was the opposite of Bentley, which is small and rural with local kids. He liked it. He made a lot of new friends, took business courses, and one in Buddhism. Then he got to travel to Indonesia, Vietnam, Thailand, Japan, and mainland China. "There were a lot of people from Europe taking a year off and most of the friends I made were from England and France. We met tourists from everywhere, including lots of Russians." He didn't get homesick, but he wasn't sure he'd like to live abroad. He still wanted to go into business, though now he had narrowed the field to accounting. "I have an internship at Price Waterhouse this summer so that will be good experience."

Sean's Mohawk hair had grown out to be a curly mane

cascading from his forehead down his neck to his upper back. He told me it was a curiosity to Asians who never think black hair will be thick and curly like that. Still, true to his basic reserve, he didn't want me to take a side-view photograph of him. When I asked why, he said he really couldn't say. He just didn't. Who would want to argue with that?

— • —

Sean graduated and took a job at Price Waterhouse that following summer. I thought it was appropriate that I end with his interview as I think he is not unusual in his generation to consider business as the best career option. The country has changed in the last couple of decades and options for young people have shifted. Finance and the circulation of global monies seems very much on the minds of young people like Sean who have the good fortune of a college education.

POSTSCRIPT

IN 2001, Robert Putnam wrote *Bowling Alone,* a study
showing how Americans live increasingly isolated and socially
disconnected lives at the beginning of the twenty-first century.
Most people by now are aware of the trends he documented:
fewer Americans go to church and or attend club meetings;
a large percentage of citizens are not politically involved;
fewer Americans entertain at home; fewer play sports though
more watch sports on TV than ever before; and small-group
activities such as card-playing and team bowling are almost
nonexistent.

I thought about Putnam's book while conducting the interviews for this book. After all, I had begun the project with
a desire to feel more connected to my neighbors—to know
them and more about their lives. Were Putnam's conclu-
sions true of myself and my neighbors? Had social isolation
increased even more now that we are in the second decade of
the twenty-first century, or was the trend starting to reverse

itself? There were no quantified answers to these questions, but I did come up with two observations.

First, I noticed how almost all of the people I talked to seemed to at least *identify* themselves with the neighborhood, if only as observers or critics. Many expressed a sense of pride in where they lived. After all, the South End has had a rich and colorful history. It has preserved valuable architecture and beautified its streets and parks. Recently it has attracted an arts community, contributing to the cultural vitality of the whole city. The South End in many ways has led the way toward more open attitudes on sex and gender identity, and above all, it has sustained a cultural and ethnic diversity that few other Boston neighborhoods can claim.

But while these were factors to be admired, the elephant in the room it seemed to me is a growing economic disparity that threatens to undo this extraordinary population mix. Real estate values have risen with alarming speed, with the average rent for a condominium close to $4,500 a month, and the average selling price for a two-bedroom condo close to $2 million. Prices for a whole house range from $2 million to $5 million, depending on the condition. Furthermore, while the median household income of the neighborhood is $53,000, the average income is $89,000 showing how the very high incomes are compensating for the low ones.

Of course, this reflects trends in the U.S. economy in general, but most South Enders I spoke to value the mix in the population that has existed for decades. Over the past 140 years the South End has been home to large numbers of Irish,

Lebanese, Jewish, African American, and Greek populations. Even today its population is approximately 55% white, 16% Asian, 13% Hispanic, 13% black or African American, and 2% other ethnic groups. People I talked with seemed proud that people from many different walks of life live peacefully in very close proximity to one another.

Nevertheless, most agree that this prized diversity is now being threatened. If real estate values continue to rise as they have in the last decade, the neighborhood could soon become a very different place: an economically homogenous high-income one with the middle class leaving, and the aged and poor squeezed to the fringes.

No one I talked with wanted that to happen.

ACKNOWLEDGMENTS

First and foremost I wish to thank the twenty-five South Enders who made this book possible by sharing their time and stories with me. While varying in age, background, and experience, each brought his or her own perspective to life in this era and in this neighborhood. I will always be grateful for their generosity.

Many friends and colleagues helped along the way. I may not have even undertaken the project without the encouragement of my long-standing writer friends Louise Herman and Gwen Romagnoli, as well as an initial conversation with Elsa and Tony Hill. I may not have stuck with the project had not Judith Felton, Louise Herman (again), Leslie Williams, and Judith Kidd encouraged me to continue. Toward the end of the writing, Tim Crellin and Bob Frank read the manuscript and made invaluable edits and suggestions.

Special thanks to Emily Callejas, faithful editor and coach ("Mom, just keep going") and to Sam Potts whose expert copy editing and graphic design gave the book its final professional form. And always thanks to Gardiner Hartmann.

Made in United States
North Haven, CT
03 November 2021

10823378R00114